FREEDOM·FROM
DEPRESSION

FREEDOM FROM DEPRESSION

JAMES E. JOHNSON

haven books
Division of Logos International
Plainfield, N.J. 07060

All Scripture passages are taken from The Living Bible, copyright © 1971 by Tyndale House Publishers, Wheaton, Illinois, unless otherwise indicated KJV (The King James Version), Phillips (The New Testament in Modern English by J.B. Phillips), or NEB (The New English Bible).

FREEDOM FROM DEPRESSION
Copyright © 1980 by Logos International
All rights reserved
Printed in the United States of America
Library of Congress Catalog Card Number: 80-84851
International Standard Book Number: 0-88270-494-X
Logos International, Plainfield, New Jersey 07060

To the staff of Philhaven Hospital, a facility established for the care and treatment of emotionally disturbed individuals. The tender, loving care so generously provided by Philhaven's dedicated practitioners offers healing to many depressed individuals.

The administration, board of directors, and the Lancaster Conference of the Mennonite Church are hereby commended for providing this facility which is devoted to healing in a Christian context.

Contents

Introduction

The shrill ring of the telephone pierced the night, interrupting the peaceful sleep of our entire household. My wife, a lighter sleeper than I, jumped out of bed and picked up the telephone. "It's for you, Jim. Someone at the hospital."

I stumbled out of bed, grasped the telephone, and blurted out a weary "hello."

"This is Philhaven Hospital calling, Mr. Johnson. It's 2:00 A.M. You are to call Mr. Ronald Jones to see about admitting his wife. She is intensely depressed, and the family feels she needs help right away."

I called Mr. Jones, who anxiously related some details concerning his wife's problem. "Our son died four months ago in an automobile accident, Mr. Johnson." His voice cracked as he spoke, but he bravely continued after regaining his composure. "Our family hasn't been the same since John was killed. My wife has taken John's death especially hard—she can hardly eat and has difficulty sleeping. We need help right away, because my wife is threatening to harm herself. Can you help us?"

I made arrangements to meet Mr. and Mrs. Jones at my office, kissed my wife good-bye, and stepped out into a cool, crisp night. Our bleak neighborhood and the damp night air brought a shiver as I longed to return to my warm, comfortable bed. I blinked to get myself fully awake as the sound of my own voice broke the silence, "It's tough to leave home on a night like this—but I'm glad the Jones family called for help rather than letting Mrs. Jones's depression get worse."

Mrs. Jones represents one of the largest groups of people who seek help from counselors—depressed individuals. Depression is sometimes referred to as the "common cold" of emotional problems, since discouragement is likely to strike most of us at some time. In fact, some sources estimate that as many as 9,000,000 Americans suffer from depression.

Unfortunately, comparing depression and the common cold ends with a statement related to their commonality. Doctors prescribe rest and aspirin for a cold, but these simple prescriptions do not eradicate depression. A cold generally runs its course in a week; depression may linger for weeks, months, or years. Furthermore, it is highly acceptable to catch a cold—nobody will think less of you if you have a case of the sniffles and sneezes. However, a terrible stigma still surrounds emotional problems, so that seeking help for depression is not nearly as acceptable as visiting the doctor for the relief of a physical illness. Furthermore, many Christians are firmly convinced that born-again believers really have no cause to be depressed.

Emotional and physical problems also differ in the intensity and kind of pain they inflict upon suffering individuals. People who come for counseling readily acknowledge that the turmoil of depression surpasses the suffering of most physical illnesses. The cancer of the soul and spirit represented by depression gnaws away with an intensity that is comparable to cancer that attacks the body.

This book attempts to confront the mystique, misunderstandings, and stigma surrounding depression. We further endeavor to cover areas rarely touched on in Christian literature regarding depression. In addition to describing the causes, symptoms, and treatment of deep discouragement, we have included material regarding childhood depression. The phenomenon of suicide, a problem which is frequently ignored in Christian circles, is also dealt with. This book is solidly built on a scriptural foundation—you will discover the life experiences of biblical characters who wrestled with depression interwoven throughout the manuscript.

Freedom From Depression has been prepared with two goals in mind. First and foremost, this book has been designed to assist believers who walk through the valley of discouragement. A second purpose is to present helpful information and suggestions to those who deal with depressed individuals.

This book is enriched by personal examples from the author's experience in dealing with depressed individuals. These illustrations are drawn from activities conducted in a wide range of clinical settings and geographical locations. Personal data has been carefully altered to conceal the identity of individuals who seek help for their problems.

A message of hope rings throughout the pages of this manuscript. The following testimony of David, a biblical character who encountered depression, is symbolic of the declaration of assurance this book endeavors to convey to all who are discouraged:

Yea, though I walk through the valley of the shadow of death, I will fear no evil: for thou art with me; thy rod and thy staff they comfort me. Thou preparest a table before me in the presence of mine enemies: thou anointest my head with oil; my cup runneth over. Surely goodness and mercy shall follow me all the days of my life: and I will dwell in the house of the Lord for ever. (Ps. 23:4-6, KJV)

FREEDOM FROM DEPRESSION

A Nice Christian Like You with a Depression Like This?

"Is everybody happy?" asked the preacher, peering out over a sea of faces. "If you're happy, why don't you tell your face about it? Smile! Why are all of you looking so glum? Don't you know that Christians are supposed to be happy people?"

Everyone in the group put on an artificial smile, doing their best to look cheerful. The leader continued, "If you're not happy, raise your hand and tell us about it so we can pray for you." People sat frozen in their seats in stony silence as tension hung heavily over the group. If anyone was sad or discouraged, he wasn't about to admit it in that particular situation.

I recently entered an office at our hospital where several staff members were discussing their work. These individuals expressed great astonishment over the number of depressed Christians who were being cared for in our facility. Someone said, "I have been taught that Christians were always happy people. I am literally amazed to discover that this is not the case."

Happiness is widely considered to be the norm for Christians. We should be cheerful, we are told, since joy is a fruit of the Spirit that should be growing in a Christian's life. However, Christians are placed in a double bind by people who insist that believers should always be happy. A person just isn't being "spiritual" when he or she is sad or discouraged.

Why do we always expect Christians to be bubbly and joyful? Are we different from biblical characters who encountered discouragement—individuals such as Job, David, and Naomi? Even Jesus Christ experienced sadness, for He is described as "a man of sorrows, and acquainted with grief" (Isa. 53:3, KJV). Jesus wept over the death of His friend Lazarus and shed tears because of the rebellion of the people of Jerusalem. He felt the press of discouragement in the Garden when He prayed, "Let this cup pass from me" (Matt. 26:39, KJV). Jesus identifies with us in times of sadness, because He also endured the pressure of discouragement.

God created us with a capacity to experience various moods and feelings. Our emo-

2

tions may fluctuate from happiness to sadness, from love to anger. We can experience peace and tranquility, or sink into times of anxiety and tension.

Why not be honest and admit that Christians do not always live on a happy plane? There are valleys as well as mountaintops in a believer's life. Joy and happiness are likely to intermingle with sadness and discouragement. Therefore, understanding the dynamics of depression helps us cope more effectively when discouragement knocks on our door.

Depression is a feeling tone of sadness, generally brought on by a loss, disappointment, or frustration. Deep discouragement is the number-one problem dealt with in counseling as therapists' offices are literally besieged by depressed people. In addition, Christians are not immune to depression, as a large portion of Christian counselors' caseloads generally consist of discouraged believers. However, this is only the tip of the iceberg, as many people who are depressed never consult a professional counselor.

Many well-known and highly respected biblical characters experienced depression. Listen to the words of Jonah in a time of discouragement, "Please kill me, Lord; I'd rather be dead than alive" (Jon. 4:3). Elijah, following a victory over Baal's prophets, became depressed to the point where he no longer wanted to live. Elijah was extremely upset when he proclaimed, "I've had enough. . . . Take away my life. I've got to die some time, and it might as well be now" (1 Kings 19:4).

David suffered acute discouragement, which is reflected many times throughout the Psalms.

Jeremiah, the weeping prophet of Israel who was known for his sadness, declared: "What sadness is mine . . . oh, that I had died at birth. . . . Lord, you know it is for your sake that I am suffering. . . . I have not joined the people in their merry feasts. I sit alone beneath the hand of God" (Jer. 15:10, 15, 17).

In a time of extreme discouragement over the stubbornness and rebellion of the people of Israel, Moses asked the Lord to kill him. "Why pick on me, to give me the burden of a people like this? . . . I can't carry this nation by myself! The load is far too heavy! If you are going to treat me like this, please kill me right now; it will be a kindness! Let me out of this impossible situation!" (Num. 11:11-15).

"Almighty God has dealt me bitter blows. I went out full and the Lord has brought me home empty; why should you call me Naomi ["pleasant"] when the Lord has turned his back on me and sent such calamity!" (Ruth 1:20-21). These are the words of a discouraged woman who had lost her husband and two sons.

New Testament characters also experienced sadness and discouragement. Peter was extremely distressed following his denial of the Lord. Overwhelmed by guilt and frustration, Judas committed suicide after he had betrayed Jesus for thirty pieces of silver. Paul wrote about being pressed down, and he mentioned a messenger of Satan buffeting him. This frustration was so severe that Paul diligently begged the Lord to remove this trial from his life (2 Cor. 12:8).

However, of all the individuals in Scripture, Job represents a classic illustration of a depressed individual. One of the wealthiest men who ever lived, Job was a multimillionaire. He was the John D. Rockefeller or J. Paul Getty of his day as far as financial gain was concerned. This immensely wealthy man owned 7,000 sheep, 3,000 camels, 500 teams of oxen, and 500 female donkeys (Job 1:3). Job had been "born with a silver spoon in his mouth," and he seemed to possess a King Midas touch.

A popular song of yesteryear states, "What a difference a day makes." Job discovered how one day can bring about drastic changes in a person's life. Satan unleashed his fury upon Job, stripping him of his treasure in one mighty blow. Job's life went from a fairly smooth road to a roller coaster of disaster and chaos. Job's losses in one day make the bankruptcies of the Great Depression look like peanuts. To top it off, Satan gave Job a case of boils that even caused his wife to look away with disgust and nausea. Can't you see Job as he sits on top of an ash heap, a prime candidate for a king-sized depression? Considering his circumstances, one could hardly blame Job for being discouraged. Here is a man who seemed to have many justifiable reasons to be depressed.

"Nice" biblical characters such as Job experienced depression just like "nice" Christians today can become discouraged. We can learn a great deal about living—including how to handle depression—by studying the experiences of biblical personalities. "All these things happened to them as examples—as object lessons to us—to warn us against doing the same things; they were written down so that we could read about them and learn from them in these last days as the world nears its end" (1 Cor. 10:11).

We often forget that "there hath no temptation taken you but such as is common to man" (1 Cor. 10:13, KJV). Contemporary Christians readily discover that their experiences in dueling with depression are highly similar to those of biblical characters who traversed valleys of discouragement.

Did you ever become discouraged following a miraculous spiritual victory? As strange as it may seem, we are likely candidates for a down time following mountaintop experiences. If this happens to you, you will be able to identify with Elijah, who suffered profound distress following an incredible display of God's power on Mount Carmel.

Job and Naomi represent individuals who experienced profound discouragement following the death of a loved one. People today still become bogged down with discouragement when family members or close friends are snatched away.

David was haunted by an uncontrollable madman named Saul who was intent on harming him. He represents contemporary Christians who become depressed when they are harassed by enemy forces.

Studying biblical characters who experienced discouragement offers more than a message of frustration and disappointment. A profound announcement proclaiming, "Depression Can Be Overcome" clearly sounds through the life experiences of these individuals. This report of victory over depression, which consistently rings down through the corridors of time, is the theme of this book—since distressed biblical characters overcame depression, you can do it, too.

With this message of hope clearly in mind, let us continue our journey by exploring the various causes of depression.

Why Am I So Discouraged?

There is an inherent curiosity within people that drives us to discover the root causes for a problem. Nearly every depressed person who comes for counseling asks, "What is making me so discouraged?" People in despair cry out, "If only I could understand what is making me so distressed, perhaps I could overcome this horrible depression!" Depressed people want to identify the underlying cause of their problem, so they can rip it out of their lives as one would uproot an ugly weed from a garden.

Depression would be much easier to cope with if the causes of deep discouragement could be wrapped up into neat little packages. While this is impossible, we can categorize the causes of depression into several general areas as outlined below.

1. Emotional or psychological factors which spring from within an individual.

   a. a negative self-concept
   b. self-pity
   c. anger
   d. guilt
   e. fear
   f. identity struggles
   g. striving for perfection

2. Environmental or external influences—forces and pressures which impinge upon an individual from the outside.

   a. depression arising from loss
   b. changes in environment or life style
   c. loneliness
   d. being pulled apart by opposing forces
   e. family stress

3. Spiritual problems—a break in one's relationship with the Lord.

The following chapters explore the causes of depression as outlined above, beginning with forces springing from within an individual.

Emotional Factors and Depression

1. A negative self-concept contributes to discouragement.

Depressed people generally do not like themselves. They are stuck in a vicious circle of focusing on negative qualities rather than recognizing the gifts God has given them. They compare themselves unfavorably with other people and reject the way the Lord has constructed them physically, emotionally, and mentally.

"Why did you come here to try to help me," a fifty-five-year-old depressed lady named Martha said to her family. Martha's negative self-concept emerged as she looked her children in the eyes and said, "You know I'm not worth anything. I've never been a good mother to you or a decent wife to your father. I'm lost, hopeless, and I'll never be any good. There is no point in your coming in for counseling to try to help me."

Martha's feelings of self-worth were almost nonexistent as she was trapped in a pattern of running herself down. Reassurance from her family regarding her positive attributes seemed to bounce right off, unable to penetrate the barrier of a negative self-concept she had wrapped about her.

Job rejected himself in a manner very similar to Martha. He looked at himself and declared, "I am but a shadow of my former self," implying that he didn't amount to much any more (Job 17:7). Job's self-image had reached such a low point that he believed he should not have been born: "Why didn't I die at birth? Why did the midwife let me live? For if only I had died at birth, then I would be quiet now, asleep and at rest. . . . Oh, to have been still-born!—to have never breathed or seen the light" (Job 3:11-16). Further evidence that Job did not think he was worth very much is indicated by this statement, "My life is but a breath, and nothing good is left" (Job 7:7). However, the clinching testimony indicating Job's negative self-concept emerges as he states, "I despise what I am" (Job 9:21).

Christians who suffer from depression stemming from a negative self-image need to realize their value to God. Your self-worth will surely be enhanced by recognizing that you are created in the image of God. Didn't He pronounce all that He created as good? Is it right to run yourself down in the light of that pronouncement?

It also helps to realize the Lord's care over you when you are discouraged. You are of more value than the petite sparrow or the majestic lily that He cares for so tenderly. "And if God cares so wonderfully for flowers that are here today and gone tomorrow, won't he more surely care for you, O men of little faith?" (Matt. 6:30).

Christians who wrestle with depression springing from a poor self-image can also be helped by recognizing who they are in Jesus Christ. Your spirits can be lifted by realizing you are a precious person whom Jesus died for. When God looks at you, He sees beyond the negative elements and views the image of His beloved Son within you. He elevates you above sin and depravity by making you a king and a priest. "[Thou] hast made us unto our God kings and priests," we read in Rev. 5:10 (KJV). How can you continue to downgrade yourself when you are worth so much in God's sight?

2. *Self-pity causes depression.*

Many Christian counselors believe selfpity is the major cause of depression. We beckon for discouragement to join us by allowing self-pity to rule our lives. We flirt with depression by nursing attitudes such as: "Poor me. Look how bad I have things. Nothing ever turns out right for me."

A depressed lady named Joan seemed to have everything going for her. Joan had raised a family of fine Christian children and had a good work record. Her husband and children testified to her success as a wife and mother. However, Joan had been depressed for several weeks and spent massive chunks of time in bed. "Just leave me alone. My life is over," Joan said to me. "I will never be any good and nobody cares about me. I have been sick for several months and no one has even come to visit me."

The self-pity which Joan allowed to invade

13

her life caused her to sink deeper and deeper into depression. She felt sorry for herself because she was sick and pitied herself because she believed people were neglecting her. This lady with considerable potential for productive living had allowed self-pity to totally blind her to the positive qualities in her life.

"I try as hard as I can, but nobody ever recognizes what I do," a man named Jack said to me. "Why doesn't someone in my family appreciate all I'm doing for them? I really have it rough at home, Mr. Johnson." Self-pity had engulfed this man who had a strong yearning to be needed and to be constantly recognized as the center of attention. However, his feelings of self-pity caused his family to turn away in disgust as they became weary of hearing him complain. Therefore, feeling sorry for himself had cut Jack off from his family rather than gaining the affection he sought from his loved ones.

"Nobody has problems like I do" is often heard by counselors dealing with depressed individuals. We open ourselves to self-pity and depression when we feel God is treating us more harshly than anyone else. When such feelings come our way, we need to realize our problems are not unique or drastically different from other people's experiences. The

Scripture that declares, "There hath no temptation taken you but such as is common to
man" means we are all in the same boat,
subject to the same contrary winds as we sail
the sea of life (1 Cor. 10:13, KJV).

Self-centered pity is characteristic of childhood rather than adult maturity. This pattern causes us to zero in on our problems and
feelings, forgetting about other people's needs.
Therefore, individuals who are locked into
self-pity need to learn to minister to other
people as a positive step toward breaking out
of their discouragement.

The compelling power of self-pity as a contributing factor in depression is frequently
portrayed dramatically in a counselor's office.
Depressed people are generally highly skilled
at pulling others into their self-pity patterns,
gaining attention and recognition through
their self-pity. For instance, Ray, a forty-nine-
year-old man who was extremely depressed,
pulled at his family's heartstrings as a counseling session began. Ray was in excellent
physical condition, but, in spite of this, he dove
right into a list of his imagined physical complaints. "I am sure I have cancer of the stomach," Ray said. "I won't be with you kids much
longer. I hope you don't grieve too much when
I'm gone." Ray completed his discourse by
announcing to his family that he probably

wouldn't last through the rest of the month.

Exploration of Ray's relationship with his family revealed they were rapidly pulling away from him. Ray's children stated, with profound feeling, "Dad only wants to talk about himself. He never inquires about any of us or seems interested in what we have to say. We get tired of hearing his complaints, especially since he's been telling us he's going to die for years."

An obvious task of counseling for a person like Ray is to help him focus his interest and attention on other people. A family which is willing to be involved in counseling is also helpful in turning around self-pity communication patterns.

Self-pity is evident in the experiences of several biblical characters who encountered depression. Job invited his friends to "pity me, for the angry hand of God has touched me. Why must you persecute me as God does? Why aren't you satisfied with my anguish? Oh, that I could write my plea with an iron pen in the rock forever" (Job 19:21-24).

Self-pity usually overtakes us when things don't go our way. We feel sorry for ourselves when the plans we have made ever so carefully somehow never work out.

Jonah is a classic example of self-pity as he became upset with the Lord when God changed

His plans regarding Nineveh. Jonah had the destruction of Nineveh all mapped out. He was the center of attention marching through that city telling everyone, "Repent, because God is going to destroy this city."

The people of Nineveh readily responded to Jonah's ministry, as they repented with sackcloth and ashes. Revival fires were burning, so God changed His mind and called off the city's destruction. What a letdown this was for Jonah. A situation that called for rejoicing had brought forth depression as Jonah complained because God did not destroy Nineveh. The Scripture describes Jonah's self-pity in this way: "So Jonah went out and sat sulking on the east side of the city, and he made a leafy shelter to shade him as he waited there to see if anything would happen to the city" (Jon. 4:5).

Sometimes Christians need to be confronted with their indulgence in self-pity. God met Jonah's self-pity head on, pointing out that it was His prerogative to save Nineveh from destruction. As the book of Jonah ends, God is telling His prophet not to be so distressed because He spared Nineveh from destruction.

3. *Problems dealing with anger cause depression.*

Depressed people are usually angry individuals. However, people who are depressed generally react to the suggestion that they are angry with: "No way! I am not an angry person. I don't harbor anger toward anyone inside of me."

A Veterans Administration hospital I once worked in employed an interesting technique to bring out repressed hostility. Severely depressed men were given very tedious, monotonous tasks far beneath their ability. The goal of this treatment was to help depressed veterans get in touch with the immense amount of hostility they had locked in or directed toward themselves.

A dentist was admitted to our unit with a severe depression. Dr. Andrews was emaciated and run down, virtually a physical wreck from running day and night to serve patients who had little mercy on him. His office records were in shambles, and many of his clientele owed large, unpaid bills from a backlog of services. The pressures of such a disorganized practice resulted in a massive depression for Dr. Andrews.

Operating on the hunch that Dr. Andrews was feeling angry over being put upon by his clientele, we gave him the job of cleaning messy ashtrays with a toothbrush and a small cloth. (It may be hard to appreciate how miserable such a task can be unless you imagine fifty men spitting and placing butts, gum, candy wrappers, and other useless items in the ashtray.) We discovered that Dr. Andrews was highly skilled in covering up any anger he might have boiling underneath. Each day for the first week when I asked him how his assignment was going, he replied, "Just great, Mr. Johnson. I love polishing and shining up the ashtrays on the unit." However, I soon noticed Dr. Andrews was not quite as thrilled about his assignment the second week. Finally, after about three weeks of such menial and miserable labor, Dr. Andrews let me know in no uncertain terms that he did not appreciate cleaning ashtrays. "I refuse to clean any more ashtrays—give me a job where I can use my abilities more fully," he said.

Unlocking his hostility over the monotonous job we gave him allowed Dr. Andrews to begin discussing his anger toward patients who had pulled him in a hundred directions. Of course, his therapy also included discussion about how he had allowed himself to be manipulated by the public. Dr. Andrews overcame his depression, and being honest about his anger was a major step in his recovery.

Individuals who are depressed find it easy to deny their hostility, because they usually push angry feelings deep down within themselves. Consequently, their hostility is directed toward themselves rather than being discharged through socially appropriate channels such as work, prayer, and open discussion of angry feelings.

I had been counseling for some time with a young lady named Betty when a problem arose in our relationship. I totally forgot an appointment I had made with Betty because I was busily engaged in another activity. Betty was seething with anger as she waited for me to appear. When I invited Betty to discuss her feelings about the mistake I made she replied, "It's OK. I'm not really mad at you. I realize things like this can easily happen."

I pushed further to ascertain Betty's true feelings rather than taking her statement at its face value. The anger she had locked inside soon came tumbling out. We were able to reestablish a positive working relationship as Betty learned to deal with her feelings. This led into further discussion regarding the ways Betty repressed angry feelings. Understanding the destructive nature of bottling up feelings inside helped Betty unlock her anger and take steps toward overcoming depression.

We can identify with individuals in the

Scripture who had difficulty dealing with their emotions. For instance, Jonah acted on his feelings rather than talking them over. The Scripture indicates that Jonah was afraid to go to Nineveh, so he fled from the Lord (Jon. 1:3). Rather than talking over his feelings with God, Jonah attempted to elude God by boarding a ship going in the opposite direction. The Lord had to get Jonah into a place where he could talk things over with His servant before anything could be accomplished in Jonah's life.

Jonah represents many people who keep running from their problems and backing away from their emotions. Individuals who try to flee from their feelings often appear in counselors' offices. For instance, Joe was a depressed young man who kept running from his true feelings, using a great deal of denial to cover up his anger and hostility. Every time a counselor touched on Joe's emotions, he would run and seek help elsewhere. Denying his emotions by running from himself was a major contributing factor in Joe's depression.

The natural flow of events often transforms self-pity into anger. It is easy to get angry along with feeling sorry for ourselves when our plans go awry. Hostility boils within when events do not turn out the way we believe they should. Jonah was intensely furious as he sat under a bush, pouting and sulking because God had foiled his plans regarding Nineveh. The Lord recognized Jonah's indignation and asked the prophet, "Is it right to be angry about this?" (Jon. 4:4). How much better it would have been for Jonah to discuss his feelings with the Lord rather than harboring and nursing anger within himself.

The Bible gives a workable formula for dealing with anger in Eph. 4:26-27: "If you are angry, don't sin by nursing your grudge. Don't let the sun go down with you still angry—get over it quickly; for when you are angry you give a mighty foothold to the devil."

There is a "do" and a "do not" in this biblical prescription for handling anger. The "do not" instructs Christians to avoid nursing their hostility by locking it inside. Christians should not bottle their anger inside themselves by fretting and stewing over an upsetting situation. Repressed hostility must be freed up and dealt with in constructive ways.

The "do" of handling anger is to get over it quickly. It is far better to talk things over with an individual we have a problem with than to nurse a grudge. Christians who go on seething with anger day after day are setting themselves up for a king-sized depression.

4. *Guilt causes depression.*

Depressed people commonly believe they pollute or ruin the lives of people they come in contact with. Their heavy load of guilt and despair may lead them to believe they have committed sins that cannot be forgiven. "I have committed the unpardonable sin" is often heard from depressed people.

Individuals suffering from depression dwell on their errors as they review their life history. They may feel guilty about being a burden to their family because they are sick. Overwhelming guilt may allow self-destruction to seem like a welcome solution to their problems.

"I have something to confess. I just know I won't be well until I rid myself of this terrible guilt," a depressed twenty-year-old girl named Barbara said to me. Barbara spent hours confessing her sin and guilt to the Lord. However, she seemed to gain little relief from such confession as she stated, "I still have a big ball of guilt down inside of me."

Counseling with a guilt-ridden individual like Barbara leads one to assume the counselee may have committed errors of mountainous proportions. I thought Barbara must have been bogged down by a sin so personal and intimate that she might never reveal the nature of her wrongdoing. However, it turned out that Barbara's guilt focused around several occasions when she angrily talked back to her parents. Counseling with this young lady and her family opened up channels of communication and reconciliation. Barbara took positive steps toward a better adjustment by realizing she could be forgiven of the behavior that had precipitated her guilt.

Depressed people who are loaded with guilt may turn to apologizing to relieve their overwhelming discouragement. I shall never forget a guilt-ridden individual who apologized for practically everything she did. After apologizing for her behavior, this individual would ask forgiveness for apologizing. She became a nonfunctioning person, as her life consisted of a series of one apology after another.

A Christian counselor has the privilege of helping people find release from guilt through spiritual resources. A non-Christian therapist tries to relieve guilt by giving advice such as "Your behavior is not wrong" or "You should not feel guilty because of what you have done." However, a Christian counselor can point to the cross of Jesus Christ, where a guilty person can lay down his burden at Jesus' feet.

Our family recently viewed a movie based on *The Pilgrim's Progress*. Pilgrim made the first part of his lengthy journey toward the Celestial City with a massive pack of sin and guilt on his back. He was bogged down at every turn by the load he carried. However, something happened to Pilgrim's weight as he knelt at Jesus' cross. Tears flooded my eyes as a hand gently lifted this heavy pack from Pilgrim's back and it went rolling down the mountain. The camera caught the load tumbling, tumbling, tumbling. Pilgrim was a free man.

It is not necessary for Christians to be bogged down with a load of depressing guilt. Jesus wants to lift that guilt package off your shoulders and set you free. Hear Him call the guilt-ridden person to "come unto me, all ye that labour and are heavy laden, and I will give you rest. Take my yoke upon you, and learn of me; for I am meek and lowly in heart: and ye shall find rest unto your souls. For my yoke is easy, and my burden is light" (Matt. 11:28-30, KJV).

5. *Fear causes depression.*

Fear and anxiety are twin causes of depression. Depressed people dread the day and often panic when morning arrives. They fear responsibility, preferring to withdraw from duties rather than handling their obligations. They are afraid of today, and the future seems to hold only perplexity and uncertainty.

One would never know there was anything wrong simply by looking into the face of an attractive twenty-five-year-old girl named Theresa. However, testimonies of fear flowed from within as Theresa spoke. Her lips quivered as she said, "I'm afraid of everything, Mr. Johnson. I'm afraid to go to bed at night, and I fear getting up in the morning. It scares me to live and I'm frightened I will die. I constantly worry that something bad will happen to my husband and children." Theresa could hardly utter a dozen words without revealing the troublesome fears that held her entire being in a viselike grip.

Fear was also a major component with each biblical character who experienced depression. Job spoke of his fear when he said, "What I always feared has happened to me" (Job 3:25). Elijah ran for his life because he was afraid that Queen Jezebel would kill him. Jonah fled in fear from the responsibility of preaching the gospel to Nineveh. David was harassed by his enemies and feared they would kill him. Peter, warming his hands by a fire, was terrified by a young lady who accused him of being one of Jesus' disciples.

We invite depression to come upon us

whenever fears creep in. Satan uses fear to pierce people like a knife. Fear does not originate from the Lord, for "God hath not given us the spirit of fear; but of power, and of love, and of a sound mind" (2 Tim. 1:7, KJV).

When you are afraid, allow these words of Scripture to sustain you: "Don't worry over anything whatever; tell God every detail of your needs in earnest and thankful prayer, and the peace of God, which transcends human understanding, will keep constant guard over your hearts and minds as they rest in Christ Jesus" (Phil. 4:6-7, Phillips).

3

In Pursuit of Life's Meaning

How can I understand myself better? What is my purpose in life? Where will I be five years from now?

These mind-boggling questions racing through a discouraged person's consciousness underscore the identity struggle that commonly accompanies depression. Individuals who are attempting to discover a purpose for living are frequently more prone to depression than people whose goals are well-defined. In fact, researchers have discovered that the incidence of depression is highest among teens, young adults, and the aged—life stages where identity crises are most severe.

"I have worked on six different jobs in the past year," said a depressed husband and father who could not find himself vocationally.

"I graduated from college, and it's really frustrating not to locate a job in my field," said a young lady who was working as a waitress.

"I'm just a housewife," states a lady who is trying to discover her identity.

Teen-agers who struggle with their futures ask, "How can I discover God's will for my life?"

Seventeen-year-old Ron, a perplexed young man who had attempted suicide, had a discouraged note in his voice when he said, "I don't know who I am. It is frightening to realize that I will graduate from high school in a month. I am confused about my goals and don't know which way to turn. Should I get a job, or would vocational school or college be best for me?"

Contemporary young people live in a pressure cooker. Undue stress is placed upon adolescents to develop their identities at a tender age. High school freshmen and sophomores are expected to indicate occupational goals by declaring an interest in college prep courses, vocational areas, or business education.

We should all deplore the subtle pressure which says to adolescents, "You have to decide what field you want to enter by age sixteen!" How ridiculous! Teens who are too young to vote are requested to make binding decisions about their futures. Did you know what you planned to do when you were sixteen years old? Are you still in the field you aimed for as a teen? How can we expect young people to make sound vocational decisions at a time when they are bombarded with perplexities related to their budding physical development, sexuality, peer group relationships, separation from home, and a host of other developmental issues? No wonder adolescents become depressed when they are faced with identity crises.

Identity struggles are not limited to young adults and teen-agers. In fact, when we feel we have arrived at a perfectly shaped identity, this is generally the time when God shows us something about ourselves that we still need to work on. Therefore, forming an identity is a process of maturation and development that should continue throughout life. The years from thirty-five to forty have been most productive for me as I have pulled together a number of insights about myself as a person.

However, it is sad when older adults cannot place their life purposes in proper perspective. "I am struggling with my calling in life," a forty-year-old man named Mark stated. "I keep questioning what makes me tick and what type of work I am cut out for. I was married, but my wife divorced me because I couldn't settle down on a job. I'm now working as a janitor even though I have a college education. I came for counseling to see if you can help me gain new directions for my life."

"I'm going fishing!"

The disciple Peter presents a pathetic picture of a middle-aged person who was caught up in an identity struggle following his denial of the Lord. This disciple who miserably fell flat on his face displayed confusion and bewilderment about his future direction. Looking at his plight as a wayward disciple, Peter cried with despair, "I'm going fishing!"

We can comprehend Peter's confusion by taking some liberty to read between the lines. It is not unrealistic to assume that Peter was severely mixed up about his life purpose at this critical time in his career. A painful awareness that he had denied the Lord three times probably precipitated thoughts such as, "I am a failure as a disciple. How can someone who makes so many dumb mistakes ever be any good to the Lord? Jesus said He would make me a fisher of men, but I'll never be able to catch anyone for Him!"

Did you ever feel that way? It seems that the whole world is against you; you're up against a wall; you don't know which way to turn! In that discouraging moment, out of a sense of deep awareness that he was a nobody, Peter naturally gravitated to the activity he knew best—fishing.

Fortunately, the fish were not biting well that particular night. After fishing for hours, the disciples didn't even have one fish to show for their effort. Imagine how frantic Peter must have felt about his identity at this point—now he couldn't even catch fish! It would be natural for him to wonder, "What *can* I do right? Is there anything I was cut out to do?"

Jesus came along just in time to rescue Peter and give him a renewed identity and sense of direction. Jesus affirmed Peter as a successful fisherman by filling his nets with a multitude of fish. Jesus instructed the disciples to "throw out your net on the right-hand side of the boat, and you'll get plenty of them!" (Notice that the Lord knew how important it was that Peter be affirmed as a competent fisherman—Peter's sense of identity needed to be enhanced.) The disciples did as the Lord instructed, and it was impossible to pull the nets in because they were so loaded down with fish (John 21:6).

After dining with His disciples, Jesus asked Peter a provocative question. "Simon, son of John, do you love me more than all else?" (John 21:15, NEB). Jesus cut directly to the heart of Peter's identity crisis by asking His disciple if he loved Him more than fishing. Through these questions, Jesus again affirmed Peter as a worthwhile fisher of men.

A metamorphosis was about to take place. Seeds were planted which would spring into full bloom when Peter became the leader of the early church. However, without Jesus' encouragement, Peter might have spent the rest of his life fishing, and the church would have been robbed of a powerful dynamo.

Peter left his nets for the second time, buoyed up by Jesus' confidence in him. Read Peter's powerful sermon on the Day of Pentecost to realize that this disciple put it all together again. If there is any further doubt, listen to Peter's positive affirmation of his position in Jesus Christ: "You have been chosen by God himself—you are priests of the King, you are holy and pure, you are God's very own—all this so that you may show to others how God called you out of the darkness into his wonderful light. Once you were less than nothing; now you are God's own. Once you knew very little of God's kindness; now your very lives have been changed by it" (1 Pet. 2:9-10).

What is man?
Depressed people who are struggling with

their identities ask questions such as "Who am I? Why did God put me on earth? What is God's will for my life?" Their searches for meaningful identity are encompassed in David's provocative question, "What is man that thou art mindful of him? and the son of man, that thou visitest him?" (Ps. 8:4, KJV).

David answered his question about man's identity with a response designed to help Christians struggling with their life purposes. He stated that we are created "a little lower than the angels . . . crowned with glory and honour. . . . to have dominion over" all of God's creation (Ps. 8:5-6, KJV).

There are three keys in this Scripture to unlock identity crises and help you discover who you are:

1. *You are created a little lower than the angels.* Think of the ability, power, and majesty of angels. Then realize that man's vital position in God's creation is only one step lower than that of angelic creatures.

2. *Man is crowned with glory.* God gave man the highest seat of honor in His earthly creation. He demonstrated His love for people by giving His Son to restore us to the lofty position originally reserved for man in Eden's garden.

3. *Man is created to have dominion over all of God's creation.* God has given this lovely

world He created as a gift for man to appreciate and enjoy.

A relationship with God through His Son Jesus Christ is the key to an identity crisis. Jesus, the light of the world, lights up your life and provides illumination for your pathway. Many who have found Him testify that "once I was lost [wandering around in confusion], but now I am found; once I was blind [groping in darkness], but now I can see."

Jerry was a young man who found himself through a relationship with Jesus Christ. Jerry's life was in complete disarray when he sought counseling for his depression. Long hair that needed washing, a scruffy, uneven beard, dark circles under his eyes, and tattered clothes highlighted Jerry's features. His appearance told of a young man who had traveled the circuit, searching for something real and lasting. Alcohol, drugs, crime, and two unsuccessful marriages lay behind as Jerry was trapped in the revolving door of identity confusion. Jerry cried out for something or someone to lead him out of the darkness surrounding him.

Jerry was introduced to the Master in one of Philhaven Hospital's foster homes. A Christian couple took Jerry into their home and gently showered God's love upon him. *Agape* love melted down the hardened barriers and walls in Jerry's life, helping him realize God had provided a light to dispel the darkness which surrounded him on every hand.

You should see Jerry now—a physical, mental, and spiritual transformation has occurred in his life. Jerry freely testifies of God's love, and he is in the process of developing a Christian drop-in social center for young people. When I recently asked Jerry what happened to him, he summarized his transformation with a paraphrase of the words of the apostle Paul: "I am a new creature; old things have passed away, behold all things have become new" (2 Cor. 5:17).

4

Common People in a Super-Duper World

A perfectionistic personality shoots people toward depression like an arrow propelled toward a bull's eye. An almost guaranteed method of producing depression is to adopt standards of performance far beyond your ability to achieve. Christians who set unattainable standards of excellence are likely to be crippled by overwhelming depression whenever they fall short of their goals.

Perfectionistic tendencies, so prevalent in depressed adults, generally have their roots in childhood experiences. In some cases, the stage is set for this process from the moment of birth. For instance, parents commonly sense an onrush of gratification and delight that accompanies the creation of a new life. Almost from the beginning you can sense a strong flavor of parental pride and accomplishment that says, "Our baby is very special. In fact, our new infant is the nearest thing to perfection that we have ever seen."

Such warm feelings upon the birth of a child are quite justifiable and understandable. For instance, I vividly recall the first time I saw each of our children. Tears welled up in my eyes as I realized the significance of new life that emanated from our marriage. Pride such as I never experienced before flooded my being as everything within me told me that these were very special children. No one could possibly have convinced me that ours were not the most wonderful babies ever to inhabit an obstetrics unit. Other infants were red-skinned and bald, but ours featured perfectly smooth, white complexions and just the right amount of hair. The other babies were crying and wretching about, but ours were sleeping peacefully, indicating that we had obviously endowed steady nerves to our offspring. You would have been hard-pressed to convince me that anything but a future president, baseball star, or doctor had just entered the world.

If you don't believe events such as these occur, enter an obstetrics unit and listen as parents and grandparents ooh and ah over their newborn children. All parents declare emphatically that their baby is the cutest, best-formed, and obviously most intelligent in the entire group. Some parents even prescribe characteristics or abilities which are difficult or even impossible for newborn youngsters to achieve. For instance, did you ever hear a new parent say, "Did you notice how sweetly my baby smiles at me?" (Doctors state that a newborn baby's smile is probably caused from excessive stomach gas.) "He looks at us just like he knows we are his parents. Isn't he the cutest thing?"

Are these innocent babies sleeping quietly in their bassinets really perfect? At this point, the mere suggestion that a newborn baby is anything but infallible would brand you as a heretic. However, parents who ascribe perfection to their children are in for a rude awakening. A baby is a gift from God—loaded with potential and different from all others. A unique creation. A gift to be treasured. However, realism dictates that each child is also endowed with the capacity to err and is destined to make many mistakes throughout life.

Concerned parents are naturally interested in the proper growth and development of their children. However, some parents hover over every word spoken by the pediatrician, hoping against hope that their child is on a par with, or ahead of, others in his achievement level. Mother is overjoyed when baby says "da-da" or takes a few faltering steps at the precise time child-care experts proclaim these events should occur. Did you ever notice small infants sporting baseball hats or T-shirts proclaiming "I am a champ" long before they even know what a baseball or football looks like? Did you ever hear a parent proudly announce, "Our child has mastered the alphabet, learned to write his name correctly, and memorized all the nursery rhymes properly. His teachers say he's far ahead of everyone else in his group."?

High-performance expectations continue and sometimes intensify as children grow older. Therefore, numerous children become discouraged whenever they cannot measure up to their parents' hopes and dreams. For instance, mom and dad may wish for Lisa to become another Beethoven, but poor Lisa only manages to play the piano with one finger. Parents may hope that Johnny will develop the proficiency of Pete Rose, but the ball always seems to skip through Johnny's legs, and his batting average is a paltry .125. How can children such as these please their parents with performances that fall short of parental expectations? One can predict "problems ahead" when youngsters fail to measure up to their parents' ideals.

A child's predicament becomes even more discouraging if parents expect superior performance in a variety of endeavors. Many children are expected to shine in sports, score high on IQ tests, excel in academics, burn up the basketball court, twirl a baton effortlessly, and glide across the floor with ease in a graceful ballet performance. Pity the poor child who is pressured to become a power-packed carbon copy of Ty Cobb, Kareem Jabar, Van Cliburn, and Leonard Bernstein, all neatly wrapped up in one package.

Are you raising a perfectionist?

Several approaches to child rearing which may result in the development of a perfectionistic personality are outlined below.

1. *Make sure your child is vividly aware of his/her weaknesses.*

A sure-fire method for setting your child up for a perfectionistic personality is constantly to point out something negative about his behavior. If your child misses a problem on a math test, be sure to highlight his error rather than giving recognition for correct responses. When your son hits four out of five times at bat, don't mention his hits but be certain to rail at him for his out. Look observantly with a critical eye when your daughter sews a dress, for this allows you to point out faults rather than the good points of the garment. If you seize upon every opportunity to point out your children's failures, they will probably work their heads off to prove you wrong, or become discouraged and give up.

"My father always told me I wouldn't amount to anything," an attractive twenty-seven-year-old lady named Marilyn said to me. "He said I had a weak mind, and constantly compared me unfavorably with my brothers and sisters." Marilyn set sail on a lifelong venture to prove her father wrong by developing a perfectionistic personality. She pushed herself to reach the top of her college class, and became a gourmet cook and an immaculate housekeeper. Marilyn emphatically disallowed her husband's request that the children stay with a baby sitter because "Good parents always care for their own children." She developed a fiercely competitive attitude toward her younger sister, who was the apple of father's eye and the favorite of everyone in the family. Marilyn's strenuous efforts to meet high expectations eventually resulted in a disabling depression which brought her to a screeching halt.

2. *Withhold praise from your children.*
Lack of parental recognition and praise aims your child directly toward a target la-

beled "perfectionistic personality." This is accomplished by not recognizing your child's competence no matter how significant his or her achievements may be. Ignore your child's talents in sports; allow academic attainments to go unnoticed; merely utter an indifferent "uh-huh" or "yes, I see" when your child displays a creative project for your approval. In short, always withhold positive feedback from your children, for encouragement may give them a false security in their present level of achievement. Your hesitation to praise your children may result in sending your child on a lifelong journey to gain your approval.

A thirty-two-year-old woman named Michelle who suffered from profound discouragement said, "I'm a grown woman, but I am still striving to please my parents. I've tried so hard to get them to notice me, but they don't seem to pay attention, no matter what I do." Michelle went on to describe her childhood, declaring, "I studied as hard as I could, played an instrument to the best of my ability, and worked to gain mom and dad's approval in other areas. However, my parents never noticed my accomplishments no matter how hard I tried. They always forced me to try harder because there were higher goals to achieve."

Michelle attempted to be a perfect mother and wife, feeling discouragement every time she fell short of the mark. This lady became extremely upset if her house wasn't immaculate, a difficult goal to achieve with two small children romping under foot. Frustrated and confused, Michelle came for counseling, hoping to find someone who could relieve her depression.

Michelle clearly needed to learn not to be so hard on herself. I concentrated on helping Michelle lower her standards from perfectionism to realism. Michelle's husband was included in the counseling, and he displayed a cooperative attitude and motivation to help his wife out of her despair. John proved to be a real asset as he assisted his wife with housework and volunteered to care for the children. In addition, I encouraged John to acknowledge Michelle's accomplishments and abilities, as she was obviously longing for recognition and attention.

However, the real key to solving Michelle's problems was tucked away in her relationship with her parents. At first, Michelle's parents were shocked to realize that their daughter's depression had any relationship to their behavior. However, they gradually realized they had had high expectations for their children and had been short on praise. They asked

Michelle's forgiveness, and vowed to notice her accomplishments in the future. Family counseling resulted in healthier family relationships, which gave Michelle a springboard to bounce out of her discouragement.

3. *Always expect a little more from your child than he can deliver.*

Remember that everyone can always do a little bit better. Be sure to pressure your children to higher and higher achievement levels if you want them to develop perfectionistic personalities.

"I'm becoming aware that I'm never satisfied with my children's accomplishments," a thirty-two-year-old father named Roger said in a counseling session. Roger ruled the family with an iron hand, militaristically putting the children through their paces. Roger's small children were expected to accomplish tasks ordinarily reserved for older teen-agers or young adults. This father forced his children to write several pages of sentences that declared, "I will do better next time" whenever they failed their assignments.

Counseling helped Roger develop insight into his unrealistic expectations for his children, causing him to proclaim, "These open discussions we are having with the family helps me understand how hard I am on the

children. Bs or Cs on their report cards aren't
good enough—they should earn the highest
grades possible. If our son hits a double, I ask
him why it wasn't a home run." Roger took
giant steps toward new relationships in his
family as he requested their forgiveness for
unrealistic expectations and vowed to be less
hard on them in the future.

4. *Parents can produce a perfectionistic personality in their children by vicariously living
out their dreams and goals through them.*
A father who never made it big in sports
may attempt to relive his frustrating childhood and adolescence as his son shoots a jump
shot smoothly through the hoop, or races
around the bases following a mighty hit.
Mother can indirectly become the most popular girl in her class once again by pushing
her daughter into the thick of the social scene.
I must wave caution flags for myself in this
area as I interact with my children. I had a
successful career as the six-foot-five-inch
center of my school's basketball team in Rock-
land, Michigan, a little town tucked away in
Northern Michigan's woodlands. Thrills of
excitement not unlike those of my high school
days well up within me every time our son
Mark steps out on the basketball court. However, Mark is not a carbon copy of me, and his

experiences in sports will probably be vastly different from mine. Therefore, I must be cautious not to relive my earlier experiences through my son. (If you think I am preaching to myself, you are absolutely correct. I must constantly be on guard not to make my children miniature extensions of myself.)

5. *Teach your children that pleasing parents should be their number-one priority.*

Did you ever stop to reflect on how your current behavior would be viewed by your parents? Jo Ann, a woman in her late twenties, still thinks frequently about pleasing her mother. "When I cook a meal, I ask myself, 'How would mother prepare this roast?' After I clean a room, I wonder if mom would be happy with my accomplishment. I constantly think about pleasing my mother, no matter what I do."

Jo Ann's mother overshadows her in a way that makes it impossible for her to escape her mother's influence. Mother's powerful presence leaves Jo Ann mortgaged to the past, obviously lacking an ability to meet today's demands without complications from mother's expectations. Moving away from home didn't bring relief, as mother's expectations accompanied her wherever she went. Divided between ministering to her husband and children and pleasing her parents, Jo Ann encountered depression and frustration on every hand.

Parents may bring about double-bind situations by placing unrealistic demands upon their children. Sometimes promises are extracted from children during moments of intense emotion and sadness. For instance, an elderly mother laid this heavy responsibility upon her son as she clung to him for a few moments prior to her death: "John, you are the most responsible of my six children, and I am asking you to care for your father when I am gone. You know that I abhor nursing homes, and I want you to promise you will never put your father in such a place. John, will you please promise me that you'll care for your dad no matter what happens?"

John impulsively assured his mother that he would assume full responsibility for father's care as he was overcome with intense grief in her dying moments. Now John spends hours caring for his elderly father, who is senile and completely helpless.* While John is willing to give of himself to meet his father's needs, he realizes that dad's full care is

---

*I believe adult children should assume as much care as possible for their elderly parents. However, such service should be a voluntary labor of love, not a pressured responsibility.

rapidly depleting his energy reserves. John is loaded with hostility toward his siblings, who will not lift a finger to serve their father. Furthermore, John's wife and children are deprived of his attention and affection because he spends excessive time caring for dad.

John is in a classical double bind. On the one hand, he desires to spend more time with his wife and children. However, his mother's words, "John, care for your father," ring over and over in his ears, and John is overwhelmed with guilt and depression whenever he considers an alternative care plan for his father.

How Parents Can Prevent Perfectionistic Tendencies in Their Children

Here are some ideas for parents who wish to help their children avoid overscrupulous behavior patterns.

First and foremost, check your expectations for your children. The following admonition may sound elementary, but it contains a profound truth: accept your child right where he is, and don't expect any more than he is capable of producing.

Do you find yourself responding in a "yes, but" manner to this statement? Shouldn't parents expect their children to achieve?" you may ask. Of course. It is reasonable to expect your children to do their very best, but don't anticipate performances beyond their innate capacities. The key to making this concept work is tucked away in the next guideline.

Second, keep the channels of communication open between you and your children. Frank and honest communiction is the key to understanding your child's abilities and limitations. Don't hesitate to ask your child if he performed to the best of his ability in a game, test, or music lesson. This allows you to send your child a clear message that states, "I expect you to do your best, but I also realize you are not perfect."

Third, don't be afraid to praise your children. Do you enjoy compliments when you accomplish something noteworthy? Remember that children have the same innate need for approval as adults. Positive recognition of your child's strengths and accomplishments will go a long way toward preventing the development of a perfectionistic personality.

Fourth, be careful not to compare your child with others. Children constantly live with comparisons, so your child is already acutely aware of how he measures up. You can help your children recognize that they are OK just as they are by refusing to fall into the trap of making comparisons.

Look around you. Notice how many children are seeking parental favor but never receive the acclamation they desperately desire. It's no wonder that children become discouraged when their achievement level falls short of adult expectations. Take a moment to feel for the child who is expected to produce superheroics with average ability.

Helping children with this struggle requires parents and other adults who interact with children to be secure in their own identities and to possess adequate self-esteem. Read on into the next chapter to discover how these goals can be attained.

5

On Superman, the Hulk and Other Superheroes

We are living in a "super-world" where everything and everyone is expected to be the greatest. A boxer tells us, "I am the greatest." Baseball stars receive multi-million-dollar contracts for catching and hitting a ball. The most valuable player receives the lion's share of the glory, even when a victory is a total team effort.

Television also projects a clear message that says, "You should be super." Wonder Woman, Superman, the Incredible Hulk, and other such TV heroes imply that completeness means possessing power and superhuman abilities. The hidden message is, "I'm not worth much unless I can twist my body into a hundred grotesque forms, fly through the air with the greatest of ease, save people in the nick of time, and solve all mysteries in thirty minutes or less."

Where does that leave youngsters and

other individuals who realize they are less than superhuman? Depressed and discouraged. A most devastating insight comes with this realization: "I'm not a superhuman being. I'm just an average, ordinary, common person." Nobody wants to be in this boat in the world we are living in.

How do you feel about common, average, ordinary things? Would watching an "Ordinary Bowl" on TV give you as great a thrill as viewing the "Super Bowl"?

A tourist attraction in Hershey, Pennsylvania, the chocolate capital of the world, features a roller coaster called the Sooper Dooper Looper. I have never experienced the thrill of this ride (furthermore, I don't ever intend to do so). However, I understand that people who are brave enough to avail themselves of the excitement of this roller coaster are in for the thrill of a lifetime. People scream, laugh, cry, and get sick as they fly around hairpin turns, plunge down steep inclines, and turn upside down on a loop the loop.

This ride attracts many individuals because of the excitement evoked by the name "Sooper Dooper Looper." Do you think people would flock to this roller coaster if it were labeled the "Ordinary Dooper Looper"? Hershey Park could suffer serious financial reverses from this attraction if it were renamed with a label that failed to indicate an experience far beyond the ordinary.

Not long ago I was helping a carpenter construct steps for our house. He sent me to the store, requesting that I bring back "tenpenny common nails" for the project. On the way to the store I began wondering, "Why should I get *common* nails for my steps? Our house deserves something far better than *ordinary* nails to hold the steps together! Maybe the hardware store will have some extraordinary or super nails I can purchase for this job."

Those nails which seem so average and commonplace are holding my steps together. Stand on my steps and feel how solid they are. Jump if you want to. Stamp your feet as hard as you can. These steps will hold because they are bonded together with common nails. Boards would be helter-skelter, scattered all over the landscape, without nails. The steps would have no stability or strength without these pins of metal that are referred to as common nails. In short, the steps are functional because common nails hold them together.

Common pins seem almost as useless as common nails. These pins lie around in drawers, frequently showing up in remote places where they are least expected. Yet, what magnificent functions they can perform. Common pins fulfill the need when loose ends are to be joined together. A common pin is a seamstress's dream come true when she is sewing a dress or skirt. Furthermore, there's nothing better than a common pin to stick a label on a garment, allowing you to discover much-needed information at a glance.

Do you realize we have been brainwashed to view objects that are common as inferior? Interestingly enough, God consistently uses common things belonging to ordinary people to perform miracles. For instance, David designed a homemade slingshot which propelled an ordinary stone into the forehead of a giant, opening the door to a miraculous military triumph. A donkey delivered a powerful sermon to a stubborn prophet. Samson grasped the jawbone of an ass, slaying a multitude of Philistines with this seemingly useless article.

A little boy's lunch in the Master's hands exploded into a provision of food for a host of people. Ordinary water was transformed into wine which astonished the guests with its superior quality. A fish was pulled out of the sea to produce revenue for taxes. Moistened clay applied to the eyes of a blind man was used to perform a miracle which caused him to proclaim, "I can see!"

The Scriptures indicate that Jesus frequently used ordinary objects to illustrate extraordinary truths. If you were to choose an illustration from nature, would you pick a majestic eagle or a minute sparrow? Would you hold up a perfectly shaped ear of corn or a single kernel? Jesus chose the petite sparrow and the tiny kernel to illustrate spiritual truths. Objects such as flowers and trees, so easily taken for granted, were placed in the spotlight as Jesus chose common things to hammer home profound lessons.

Ten-talent, five-talent, and one-talent people

Did you ever hear a fellow believer proclaim, "I have no talents that the Lord can use." The real message behind such a statement may be that the speaker has no outstanding or extraordinary abilities that he can present to God. Such an individual may not be able to sing solos, preach sermons, play the organ, or be Sunday school superintendent. However, *everyone* has some abilities that God can use in His service.

Recently, I served as the organist for a weekend retreat that featured several speakers who possessed an array of talents and abilities. The group thrilled as a Yale graduate spoke brilliantly on the topic of "Evolution versus Creation." Everyone stood in awe of this young man's knowledge, understanding, and competence in presenting his topic.

However, the next program was remarkably different. The speaker was a former alcoholic with a grade-school education who testified that he once believed he had nothing to offer the Lord. Yet, he was willing to surrender what he possessed to God. The Lord remarkably opens doors for this man's ministry, and thousands are finding Christ as Lord through his witness. There was hardly a dry eye as the speaker told of numerous prisoners on death row whom he led to the Lord.

The speaker with a grade-school education could easily feel inferior to the Yale graduate. He could sit back and say, "I lack his education, so there isn't much I can do for the Lord." Similarly, the gentleman with the Ivy League college degree could say, "I don't have a dramatic testimony of being rescued from alcoholism, so I guess I'll just keep still." However, neither needs to feel inferior to the other, because they each have unique gifts imparted to them for use in God's service.

The Bible clearly acknowledges that each individual is blessed with unique gifts and aptitudes. Some people, the ten-talent folks, are loaded with ability in that they succeed in almost everything they do. Mr. or Mrs. Ten Talent presents a picture of completeness and near perfection that becomes the envy of everyone. People remark, "I would be happy if I could play the piano, sing solos, or accomplish things for God like Mr. and Mrs. Ten Talent."

Nobody minds being a five-talent individual, for this type of person also displays moments of greatness in his service unto the Lord.

Pity the poor one-talent person, however. Ugh! He occupies a position nobody strives for. The achievements reached by the ten-talent people seem like lofty mountains that one-talent individuals can never scale. Even ascending halfway up the hillside to occupy Mr. Five Talent's position seems impossible for the one-talent person. No wonder Mr. One Talent timidly buried his gift in the sand. People still dig graves for their talents as they sadly proclaim, "What's the use of trying, because I'll never amount to anything in God's service anyway." The hidden message in such a statement may be, "I won't do anything for God unless I can perform it perfectly."

The high premium placed on outstanding Christian service can easily cause believers to be bogged down with feelings of inferiority. Christians commonly believe they're not worth much unless they have put it all together with a public speaking or singing ministry. They may be convinced that their testimony is not worthy of attention unless they have been dramatically delivered from drug addiction, rescued from alcoholism, or healed of cancer.

Such a focus on outstanding accomplishments causes the average Christian to proclaim, "I have very little to offer the Lord unless I can do something extraordinary." A Christian lady once made this statement with a hint of anger in her voice: "Christians who testify always highlight the victories they are winning. I'm going to suggest that those of us who have some failures behind our names have equal time." Another Christian commented that the outstanding and well-known believers regularly appearing on a particular TV program made her feel inferior, for she did not have her life together as they apparently do.

I question that the Great Commission can ever be achieved by believers whose names are household words. Are battles won by the generals or by the soldiers in the trenches? The commanding officer may get the credit, but it is generally the troops on the front line who turn the tide toward victory.

Miracles with a shepherd's rod?

God suddenly and miraculously appeared to Moses in a burning bush and asked, "Moses, what is that in your hand?" Moses nearly fainted with fright, and probably was confused by God's question. He looked down at his hands and noticed that he was carrying a piece of wood—a shepherd's rod, to be exact. Moses undoubtedly wondered what a piece of wood could possibly accomplish for God, and he may have inquired, "What good is a shepherd's rod to you, Lord?"

A shepherd's rod doesn't seem like much of a gift. Simply possessing a piece of wood in the shape of a rod doesn't transform a person into a musician or an orator. A rod's usefulness is generally limited to frightening dangerous wolves or other menacing predators away from helpless sheep.

A rod to do miracles? God told Moses to use his rod to do miracles, and "then they will realize that Jehovah, the God of their ancestors Abraham, Isaac, and Jacob, has really appeared to you" (Exod. 4:1-8).

Moses seems like a one-talent individual as he stands with only a rod in hand. But God took that simple instrument to give Moses the look of a ten-talent individual. This rod was destined to turn into a snake and devour serpents created by Pharaoh's magicians.

The mighty Nile River turned to blood, dust was transformed into pesty lice, and threatening, pitch-black darkness enveloped the land as Moses' rod was stretched forth. The rod became a key instrument in gaining Israel's freedom from Egypt's oppressive bondage.

The apostle Paul summarized God's intervention in the affairs of men in this way: "Notice among yourselves, dear brothers, that few of you who follow Christ have big names or power or wealth. Instead, God has deliberately chosen to use ideas the world considers foolish and of little worth in order to shame those people considered by the world as wise and great. He has chosen a plan despised by the world, counted as nothing at all, and used it to bring down to nothing those the world considers great, so that no one anywhere can brag in the presence of God" (1 Cor. 1:26-29).

A great man who possessed a load of love for the average person in this world once said: "God must really love the common people, because he made so many of us." You might be a common person, but you are precious to God who says, "You are a chosen race, a royal priesthood, a dedicated nation, and a people claimed by God for his own, to proclaim the triumphs of him who has called you out of darkness into his marvellous light. You are now the people of God, who once were not his people; outside his mercy once, you have now received his mercy" (1 Pet. 2:9-10, NEB).

Fear of making a mistake—a crippling phobia

A man named Joe consulted me for depression. He stated, "I am spiritually bankrupt, totally shipwrecked." Joe had a history of active service in Sunday school and other church ministries. However, in describing an error he made approximately one year ago, Joe said, "I blew it by not taking advantage of an opportunity to serve the Lord." Joe's strong drive to be perfect caused him extreme difficulty as he attempted to erase his blunder.

Joe withdrew from Christian service as he thought about his mistake. "If I can't do anything without goofing up, I won't do it at all," he said. Joe's strong drive for perfection coupled with an inability to tolerate flaws in his nature pushed him into the throes of depression.

Many Christians are seriously impeded from effective Christian service because they are afraid of making a mistake. This hang-up is mightily used by Satan to encumber God's people from being useful servants. The devil turns this inherent fear into a crippling phobia as he whispers in our ears, "You'll make a fool of yourself if you try to do that" or "You'll surely make a mistake and everyone will laugh at you."

When will we realize God wants to bless and use what we now possess for His glory? Must we wait for some future date when our talents are polished to perfection? Remember that the Lord can compensate for your imperfections and use what you are offering for His glory. Our moments of weakness allow His strength to shine through, for "When I am weak, then am I strong" (2 Cor. 12:10, KJV). "And he said unto me, My grace is sufficient for thee: for my strength is made perfect in weakness. Most gladly therefore will I rather glory in my infirmities, that the power of Christ may rest upon me" (2 Cor. 12:9, KJV).

Shouldn't perfection be a Christian's goal? After all, the Bible tells us to "be perfect, even as your Father in heaven is perfect" (Matt. 5:48).

Through this exhortation, does Jesus imply that He expects us to live an errorless life? To the contrary. Read the context of this verse and you will discover that Christ is challenging us toward more positive relationships with other people: "Love your enemies . . . pray for them which despitefully use you" (Matt. 5:44, KJV). This passage talks about a perfect way to handle difficult problems that arise in our relationships with others. It is clear that Christ is admonishing us to strengthen our emotional well-being by praying for our offenders and relating properly to other people. Therefore, this is not necessarily a command to live an errorless existence.

Christians should set realistic goals that propel us toward completeness and maturity. We press toward perfection as we grow in grace and become more like our Lord. The "Light of the world" wishes to beam the radiance of His excellence through us to illuminate a dark, ominous world.

However, an honest self-evaluation compels us to readily acknowledge our imperfections. We will never achieve an errorless existence, no matter how hard we strive for that goal. "If I justify myself, mine own mouth shall condemn me: if I say, I am perfect, it shall also prove me perverse" (Job 9:20, KJV).

Nevertheless, a candid recognition of our imperfections never provides a valid excuse for stagnation. "I have not yet reached perfection, but I press on, hoping to take hold of that for which Christ once took hold of me. My friends, I do not reckon myself to have got hold of it yet. All I can say is this: forgetting what is behind me, and reaching out for that which lies ahead, I press towards the goal to win the prize which is God's call to the life above, in Christ Jesus" (Phil. 3:12-14, NEB).

It is easy for Christians to get caught up in extremes. We can propel ourselves toward a mistake-free existence, or drift into apathetic complacency as we realize that perfection is an unattainable goal. Choosing either end of the spectrum becomes problematic.

The Lord doesn't direct us toward passivity or request that we stop growing and maturing. He fully anticipates that Christians will develop their abilities to the greatest possible extent, but He also recognizes our human weaknesses. He loves you even though you haven't arrived at the point of perfection. God isn't looking for superheroics from you— He merely asks that you become the best person you are capable of being.

Real self versus idealized self—"I'm not what I would really like to be"

Two aspects of an individual's self-concept may declare war on each other. One of these, the idealized self, is our picture of who we would like to be. The other, the real self, is the insight we develop regarding who we actually are. A healthy self-image evolves when these two parts of our personality are harmoniously blended together.

Depression comes knocking on the door of

an individual who has a large gap between his idealized self and his real self. Problems result when you build your idealized self into perfection, but your real self falls short of that goal. For instance, you are headed for trouble if your goal is to be a doctor (idealized self) but you know in your heart that you are cut out to be a ditch digger (real self). A 110-pound weakling who wants to be a professional wrestler is probably being equally unrealistic.

Someone recently told me that stray dogs in a particular neighborhood are completely safe because the new dogcatcher is afraid of dogs. This man's ideal of being a dogcatcher is out of harmony with his realistic abilities to handle that particular position.

Depression results when the idealized self and the real self are not in unison. A sound mind results when we bring our idealized self-image in line with reality. Inner peace occurs when our goals harmonize with our abilities.

"Accept yourself as you are" sounds like a cliché, but it also contains a piece of sound advice. Individuals who enjoy self-acceptance are not pressuring themselves toward perfection. They realize God loves them just as they are. They strive to bring their idealized selves and real selves into harmony as they grow and mature. They are acutely aware of God's pronouncement of "okayness" upon them.

Jesus was talking to you when He said, "Look at the birds! They don't worry about what to eat—they don't need to sow or reap or store up food—for your heavenly Father feeds them. And you are more valuable to him than they are. . . . Look at the field lilies! . . . King Solomon in all his glory was not clothed as beautifully as they. And if God cares so wonderfully for flowers that are here today and gone tomorrow, won't he surely care for you, O men of little faith?" (Matt. 6:26-30).

You indeed are more valuable than the sparrows in the air or the lilies of the field.

6

External Factors in Depression

Emotional or psychological factors consti-
tute the bulk of material written on depression from the Christian point of view. Focusing on internal processes without a proper
understanding of external factors can lead to
an unbalanced approach in understanding
depression. A preoccupation with internal
processes means that gnawing guilt, crippling self-pity, repressed anger, and a disabling negative self-concept have all occu-
pied center stage in a description of depression's root causes.

This preoccupation with the internal processes results in a sad neglect of external factors which lead to depression. Consequently,
we are just becoming aware of how events
occurring around us can bring on discouragement.

Circumstances beyond our control frequently sting us with crushing blows. The

disheartening loss of a loved one, modifications required by changing life styles, and empty feelings brought about by loneliness may have a cruel impact upon our emotional well-being. This chapter highlights some of the external causes of depression in the form of bumps and bruises which life sends our way.

1. *Grief accompanying the loss of a precious possession contributes to depression.*

Depression can easily occur when something or someone of great value is snatched away through death, the loss of a job, or waning physical health. Surrendering a part of the body, such as the amputation of a limb, can also cause depression. In addition, discouragement can result when people who once were dear to us withdraw their affections.

Losing a family member through death often results in depression for those who bear the grief. A biblical personality named Naomi lost her husband and two sons while living in Moab. This woman returned to Judea a depressed and bitter person. The severe losses that visited her family literally shattered her world. Her friends rejoiced when Naomi came back home, but she rebuked them by saying: " 'Don't call me Naomi. Call me Mara,' (Naomi means 'pleasant'; Mara means 'bitter') 'for Almighty God has dealt me bitter blows. I went out full and the Lord has brought me home empty; why should you call me Naomi when the Lord has turned his back on me and sent such calamity!' " (Ruth 1:20-21).

An attractive and talented Christian lady named Jean sought counseling for depression. As Jean and I walked together to my office, I noticed she lacked a spring in her step and a sparkle in her eye. In giving me the history of her problem, Jean related that she and her husband had lost a baby soon after birth. This loss was difficult enough to handle. However, another child recently ran into the path of a car and was killed. Jean said, "I was somehow able to handle the death of my first baby, but losing another child in such a tragic way is more than I can bear."

While counseling is helpful to a person like Jean, it takes God's "balm of Gilead" to heal the wounds caused by such a massive loss. Jean came for counseling for several months, and her depression gradually subsided. We included her husband in the counseling process, and this was a period of dynamic growth in their relationship as they sought solace from each other. Prayer, God's healing, the support of her congregation, and counseling combined to bring healing to this person who had suffered such severe losses.

Job was an affectionate father who shepherded a closely knit family. The biblical description of Job's family interaction gives some insights into his love for his children: "Every year when each of Job's sons had a birthday, he invited his brothers and sisters to his home for a celebration. On these occasions they would eat and drink with great merriment. When these birthday parties ended—and sometimes they lasted several days—Job would summon his children to him and sanctify them, getting up early in the morning and offering a burnt offering for each of them. For Job said, 'perhaps my sons have sinned and turned away from God in their hearts.' This was Job's regular practice" (Job 1:4-5).

Job suffered severe losses as his sons and daughters were swept away by a mighty windstorm. Imagine how this devoted father felt when his children were suddenly snatched away. His wife even turned her back on him, admonishing Job to "curse God and die." Job's grief is vivid when he says, "But now my grief remains no matter how I defend myself; nor does it help if I refuse to speak. For God has ground me down, and taken away my family" (Job 16:6-7).

Job further sensed the withdrawal of his family's love and concern when he said, "He has sent away my brothers, and my friends. My relatives have failed me; my friends have all forsaken me. Those living in my home, even my servants, regard me as a stranger. . . . My own wife and brothers refuse to recognize me. Even young children despise me" (Job 19:13-18). Job further elaborates on his grief by saying, "My eyes are red with weeping and on my eyelids is the shadow of death. . . . My friends scoff at me, but I pour out my tears to God" (Job 16:16, 20).

Losing a family member through divorce or separation is also a traumatic experience that can cause depression. In fact, divorce or separation can be more difficult to deal with than death. Continued contact with a separated partner constantly opens up festering hurts and jagged wounds before they can heal. Consequently, many people who come for counseling with depression have recently gone through a marriage breakup.

Everyone in the home feels the impact when a family falls apart. The husband becomes upset because the relationship with his wife and children has been severed. A depressed young man named John came into my office with a long face and said, "I came home two nights ago from work to a bare house. The furniture was gone, and my wife and children were nowhere to be found. The house was empty and my voice echoed back to me as I cried out for my family. I have been in a state of shock ever since. I honestly don't know why my wife left me, because I thought we had a good marriage."

Women who feel a strong sense of responsibility for their family's well-being can experience considerable guilt and depression when their marriage falters. Being forced to raise children on their own without a husband places an extra burden on a mother. The guilt of a marriage failure, along with facing the future without a husband, can cause depression.

"It would have been easier for me to deal with this problem if my husband had died," a young lady named Kay said in a counseling session. Kay's husband, Tim, deserted her for another woman, and Kay was struggling over an impending divorce. "My biggest struggle is that I seem to meet Tim everywhere. I can hardly go to the shopping center or downtown without seeing him with his girlfriend. It's so hard to contact him when I know he can't be a part of my life. Each time I see my husband, it opens up hurts that still fester from our separation."

Parents often bring their children in for

counseling following a divorce or separation. Depression, school problems, retreats into a fantasy world, and fears can develop when children experience the trauma of family breakdown. Bed-wetting, crying spells, stomachaches, and thumb sucking are a few symptoms children may experience when their parents split up.

A teen-ager named Donna slashed her wrists and gulped down pills in an effort to take her life. Donna told me her frequent efforts at self-destruction were calculated to bring her separated parents back together again. "I would give anything for my family to be reunited," Donna told me.

After several futile attempts, I was able to bring Donna's separated parents in for counseling. However, Donna's mom and dad fought ferociously through counseling sessions, openly admitting they were not ready for reconciliation. One of the most touching moments I have ever experienced in counseling occurred as Donna embraced her parents, pulling them in toward her and each other. Tears flowed freely as this family held each other in a few fleeting moments of closeness and intimacy. Unfortunately, this warm interaction only lasted for a short time, as this couple was not ready to reconcile their differences and reunite the family.

Loss is an inevitable part of life that every person eventually encounters. Christians have resources through their relationship with God and each other that go far beyond what secular society offers grief-stricken individuals. The message of Christianity gives hope that fills the void created by loss. How frightening and terrifying it would be to experience bereavement without the comforting arms of Jesus, who "sticks closer than a brother" (Prov. 18:24). When death strikes, we take solace in the hope that Jesus offers: "And now, dear brothers, I want you to know what happens to a Christian when he dies so that when it happens, you will not be full of sorrow, as those are who have no hope" (1 Thess. 4:13).

We are also comforted to realize we will eventually join those who have gone before. "The believers who are dead will be the first to rise to meet the Lord. Then we who are still alive and remain on the earth will be caught up with them in the clouds to meet the Lord in the air and remain with him forever. So comfort and encourage each other with this news" (1 Thess. 4:16-18).

Here is another promise for people who are experiencing grief: "He has sent me to tell those who mourn that the time of God's favor to them has come. . . . To all who mourn in

Israel he will give: Beauty for ashes; Joy instead of mourning; Praise instead of heaviness" (Isa. 61:2-3).

2. *Changes in environment or life style can induce depression.*

Adjusting to difficult alterations in one's living arrangements or life style enhances the possibility of depression. Learning to live without one's spouse, adjusting to a smaller income following retirement, or moving from one place to another can cause depression.

I recall experiencing a period of discouragement several years ago when our family vacated a mobile home to reside in a large house. Other family members were thrilled with the move, but I became depressed. Many questions flooded my mind about the wisdom of our moving. I felt we could never pay the higher mortgage and convinced myself that we had paid too much for the new house. It was several weeks before I was able to break out of the discouragement which resulted from a major change in our living arrangements.

"Life has brought too many adjustments for me to cope with," said a fifty-five-year-old depressed woman named Ruth. Ruth had lost her husband a year before, and his death had precipitated a whole series of difficult events in her life. "I must leave the house we lived in for years, because I just can't afford to live there any longer," Ruth said. Ruth was also forced to adapt to a smaller income and had to accept employment to supplement her meager income. Such major changes in her life style caused depression to take root in Ruth's life.

There are various times when changes occur in the family life cycle that contribute to depression. Some women become depressed when a new baby arrives on the scene. While hormonal changes related to pregnancy may contribute to discouragement, the added responsibility of motherhood also adds to depression. Some mothers find it difficult to manage when the children are all attending school and no little ones remain at home any longer. Facing the "empty nest" when children reach adulthood and leave home can also be a trying time for a couple.

Probably the most difficult changes to deal with, however, involve retirement and old age. Going from a life of work to one of leisure is sometimes equivalent to being put "on the shelf" or feeling useless. Adjusting to a fixed income when inflation is rampant, dealing with health problems, and facing death are further factors that contribute to depression in older people.

How discouraging it must be to grow old and look back on a life filled with heartache and disappointment. Eli represents one of the most pathetic senior citizens whose testimonies are recorded in Scripture. Eli's older years found Israel engaged in bitter combat with the Philistine nation. The safety of God's ark depended upon the outcome of these battles. This ninety-eight-year-old blind man sat by the roadside with a trembling heart as he awaited news from the battlefield. This discouraged man undoubtedly thought back over his life, possibly recalling that he had not disciplined his sons properly. His two boys, Hophni and Phinehas, embarrassed their father by mocking the ceremonies of the Israelites and blaspheming God's laws. Suddenly Eli's contemplation was interrupted by bad news from the battlefield—his sons had been slain and the ark of God had been captured by the Philistines. This was too much for Eli's troubled mind to handle. This discouraging report made him fall backward, causing an injury that resulted in death.

David represents a contrast to Eli as he looks back on his life with many positive memories. David recalls that God was with him at every turn in the road. Psalm 71, written by David in his older years, is a precious testimony of how God accompanies His people through various life stages. David begins by recounting that God was with him when he was born. "By thee I have been holden up from the womb: thou art he that took me out of my mother's bowels" (Ps. 71:6, KJV). David's youth was also a time of closeness to the Lord, for he declared, "O God, thou hast taught me from my youth: and hitherto have I declared thy wondrous works" (v. 17).

David also pleads with the Lord not to forsake him as he enters the twilight years of life. "Cast me not off in the time of old age, forsake me not when my strength faileth" (v. 9). "Now also when I am old and gray-headed, O God, forsake me not" (v. 18).

God is with us at every stage of life. He will not leave you for "I have been young, and now am old; yet have I not seen the righteous forsaken, nor his seed begging bread" (Ps. 37:25, KJV). Christians do not have to be overcome with anxiety and depression as we experience the cycles that characterize this earthly pilgrimage. God is with us at every bend in the road and walks with us through the winding path of life's changing circumstances.

3. *Loneliness is a factor in depression.*

Loneliness is one of the most dreaded diseases of our day. We live in a very impersonal, computerized age where many people feel that they are little more than a social security number or a slot in the government's computer.

Did you ever experience loneliness in a crowd with people milling about on every side? The streets of a large city, teeming with people, can be the loneliest place on earth. My work as a consultant for a girl's home in New York City results in frequent trips to that city. I often walk on city streets, rubbing elbows with hundreds of people but still feeling lonely. The presence of many individuals merely serves to remind me of the acute loneliness of being separated from loved ones.

Our mobile society discourages the intimate and supportive family relationships that people need for good mental health. Families characteristically have loved ones scattered from coast to coast or around the world. Prolonged separation contributes to distressing loneliness and isolation.

For several years my wife and I have lived at least 500 miles from our parents. There are lonely times caused by the distance between us. We have discovered that holiday seasons when the rest of the family enjoys family gatherings are usually the most difficult.

The incidence of depression and suicide increases at holiday times when loneliness is most pronounced. Christmas is an especially difficult time for people who are far from home. Counselors often remark that their caseloads swell with depressed people who are lonely over the Christmas holidays.

Jesus Christ suffered excruciating loneliness as He approached His impending death. Jesus felt the bitter sting of loneliness as He was forsaken by His disciples who caught a few moments of sleep. The Master agonized in isolation and distress as He prayed, "Let this cup pass from me" (Matt. 26:39, KJV).

Jesus stood alone before Pilate as the jeering mob screamed for His crucifixion. Lifted high on a cross to die, He cried out: "My God, my God, why hast thou forsaken me?" (Matt. 27:46, KJV). Jesus identifies with us when we feel isolated and alone because He also experienced extreme desolation.

Have you ever felt you were the only real Christian around, and that everyone else had turned their backs on the Lord? This was Elijah's predicament as he found himself far out in the wilderness, cut off from friends and fellow believers. "I am the only one left," Elijah cried out to God in his time of loneliness.

God moved quickly to assure Elijah that he was not alone, pointing out that there were 7,000 Israelites who had never bowed their knees to Baal (1 Kings 19). Remember that the Lord is also a resource for you in your lonely moments. In addition, the support of fellow believers helps to fill the vacuum caused by loneliness. God has a special place in His heart for lonely people, as He admonishes His Church to reach out to lonesome widows, visit secluded prisoners, and comfort the bereaved.

When you are lonely, you need to realize that Jesus is a very present help in time of need. What a privilege to recognize His presence in our lonely moments, acknowledging that He will walk with us through all our tomorrows. Hear Him say to you, "I will never leave thee, nor forsake thee. . . . Lo, I am with you alway, even unto the end of the world" (Heb. 13:5; Matt. 28:20, KJV).

4. *Being pulled apart by opposing forces creates depression.*

We are living in a time when most of us are called upon to wear a number of different hats. The role demands of parenthood, marriage, employment, community, and church may crash in upon us. Such a large number of responsibilities beckoning for our time and attention can easily result in depression.

Everyone suffers when warring factors from within and without vie for our attention. Men feel the demands of work, home, and community responsibilities. Teen-agers become discouraged when high standards of attainment are expected scholastically, socially, and athletically. However, it appears that the twentieth-century woman is particularly susceptible to such problems. The explosion of female roles has removed the modern woman from her home, placing her squarely in the center of responsibility in employment, church affairs, community, and social activities. This may result in a situation where a woman is literally torn apart by a multitude of demands, and it may help to account for the fact that women who seek help for depression outnumber men who seek such help.

This problem was graphically demonstrated at a conference I once attended. A family was being interviewed by the seminar leader when the wife identified job, family, community, and church affairs as warring forces that were tearing her apart. The conference leader asked various people to represent physically the forces that were vying for this woman's attention. As several individuals tugged on her at once, it was not long before this lady was stuck and unable to move. She had to shed some of the powerful forces that had been making demands on her before she could function again.

This conference provided an impetus for me to note how many depressed people are pulled apart by opposing forces. One lady verbalized that she was caught in a war between her job, her husband, and her children. She willingly engaged in a tearful interchange with her family, explaining the many ways they were placing conflicting demands upon her. "John, you could help by keeping your room clean; Nancy, you're old enough to cook so I don't have to prepare meals every night; Jim, as my husband, you could help by disciplining the children and not leaving it all up to me." This lady's plea for help fell on listening ears, as the family engaged in a meaningful discussion about relieving discomforting stress for mother.

People who are discouraged because of multiple forces tugging at them should examine their priorities. Is it necessary for you to work, hold down an office in the club, serve on several committees, etc.? Is it even possible that overextending yourself in service to your church is bogging you down? Could you lighten your load by eliminating, cutting back, or delegating some of your responsibility to others?

"Take one thing at a time" is good advice for individuals who are caught in the vise grip of conflicting forces. Depression sets in when multiple major responsibilities impinge upon you. It may be possible that you can't eliminate or delegate all of your obligations—you can't stop being a parent or quit your job impulsively, for example. However, you can set aside some responsibilities for later, greasing the wheel that makes the loudest squeak rather than trying to take care of everything at once, ending up in a frenzy.

Here is timely advice directly from Scripture which may aid you as you labor on:

There is a right time for everything:
    A time to be born, a time to die;
    A time to plant;
    A time to harvest; ...
    A time to cry;
    A time to laugh;
    A time to grieve;
    A time to dance; ...
    A time to hug;
    A time not to hug; ...
    A time to be quiet;
    A time to speak up; ...
Everything is appropriate in its own time. But though God has planted eternity in the hearts of men, even so, man cannot see the whole scope of God's work from beginning to end. So I conclude that, first, there is nothing better for a man than to be happy and to enjoy

himself as long as he can; and second, that he should eat and drink and enjoy the fruits of his labors, for these are gifts from God. (Eccles. 3:1-13)

7

Depression Is a Family Affair

Relationships with others, particularly family members, have only recently taken their rightful place as causative factors in depression. Would you agree with my strong conviction that the most important single cause of depression is family breakdown and disintegration? A healthy family is central to every aspect of life; our nation, churches, and emotional well-being rise and fall with the fortunes of the home. Healthy family life provides a foundation for sound emotional health, but family breakdown spins off numerous kinds of pathology.

The great impact that fragmented family relationships makes on chronic depression was vividly portrayed in a job I held as a social worker in a large Veterans Administration hospital. Discovering 150 patients who had spent an average of 12.5 years in the hospital was enough to leave me stunned and horrified. Many questions raced through my mind as I surveyed this caseload of men who desperately needed my services. For instance, I wondered how many veterans had relatives who were still concerned about them. What impact does an extended stay in a large mental hospital have on family relationships?

The answers to these perplexing questions emerged as I talked with patients and put forth intense efforts to contact family members. Remorseful tears, bitter expressions of hostility, and overwhelming feelings of hopelessness and helplessness were but a few of the emotions that emerged as numerous patients related they had not heard from their families for years. Heartbreaking stories unfolded of spouses who had obtained divorces, children who had severed contact with their fathers, and parents who seemed to care very little for their hospitalized relatives. Furthermore, families related that they had symbolically "buried" their mentally ill relatives years before when they had been admitted to the hospital. The mental hospital, with its supportive staff and cast of fellow patients, became the patients' "family" as these men developed a chronic dependency on the hospital, leading to years of care at taxpayers' expense. Without a healthy family to turn to, these patients became chronically and helplessly mired down in depression and other mental disorders.

Take some time to acquaint yourself with the institutions in your community to discover the extent of depression resulting from family breakdown. Follow Christ's admonition to visit prisons and you will note that many legal offenders are embroiled in family conflict. Sense the depression of an aged individual confined to a nursing home who seldom hears from family members. Contact a children's home to share the despair of youngsters who are separated from parents. Talk with someone who works in a mental health agency, and you will discover that marriage and family problems frequently team up with emotional disorders.

It may not be necessary to search very far to discover discouraged individuals suffering from family stress. Look around you in your church group or neighborhood, and you will note that depression springing from family deterioration is closing in on every hand. Moms, dads, children, and in-laws are all candidates for profound discouragement when relationship problems creep into family systems.

The rapid descent of families headed for breakdown contains seeds of depression ready to ripen at each stage of family deterioration.

All family members are vulnerable, but children frequently bear the brunt of stress and strain emerging from troubled families. While adults often pick up the pieces of a broken relationship through relationships with other individuals, the scars of widespread family deterioration live on in the tender spirits of children.

Let us examine the process of family breakdown, paying particular attention to the resultant impact of depression on family members. We will make a special effort to examine the precarious position of children who are growing up in families with turmoil and stress.

Stage one—marital strife

This stage is characterized by marital conflict, as spouses become embroiled in destructive relationships. Fighting, arguing, and verbal and sometimes physical battles describe the interactions of spouses engaged in open warfare. The family embroiled in marital stress can be pictured by the chart on the following page. The broken line in the diagram that follows indicates a severed relationship between the spouses. Children are caught between mother and father, desperately attempting not to over-identify with either parent. Each spouse may attempt to sway the children, resulting in intense pressure and stress as children are pulled between parents. Children become mediators or referees, sometimes making heroic efforts to persuade mom and dad to reconcile their differences.

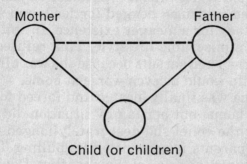

Child (or children)

This type of family frequently results in depression for spouses who are horrified as they watch their dreams for a beautiful relationship slowly erode. Equally disconcerting are the emotional problems which a child may develop from being caught in an impossible double bind between feuding parents. Stomachaches, nervous habits, sleeping disorders, learning difficulties, and sadness are only a partial list of symptoms which may emerge when children are trapped in a prison created by their parents' conflict.

Tina, a fifteen-year-old girl, came for counseling after running away from home and repeated attempts at self-destruction. Tina's parents and the legal authorities frantically sought for her during her month-long mysterious disappearance. Tina's adventure into the cold world was a nightmare as she indulged in drugs, begged for food, and sold her body for a meager existence. In spite of such a miserable life style, Tina refused to return to her parents because she was afraid her life would be even worse at home.

Tina was finally located and forced to return home, but her family situation did not offer the relief she desperately longed for. Her parents fought violently, pulling Tina right into the thick of their conflict. Depression became an escape route as Tina found she could no longer tolerate being the target of her parents' hostility or the scapegoat for family problems.

The old saying "An ounce of prevention is worth a pound of cure" applies well to families like Tina's. Couples with conflicts should not hesitate to seek counseling before problems become so acute that children run away or separation becomes a welcome relief. A marriage or family counselor can offer considerable benefit to families on the verge of problems similar to Tina's family.

Stage two—The broken home

A married couple under stress cannot survive constant pressure and may eventually separate or divorce. Relationships in the family can now be pictured in the following manner:

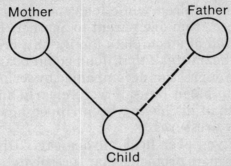

Mother　　　　　　　Father

Child

Separated parents frequently relate to each other through their offspring, creating intense pressure as they vie for their children's affection and battle over custody. Children may be forced to express a greater loyalty to one parent by being compelled to decide where they will reside. Is it any wonder that children become depressed when the family breaks up?

A staff member once conducted an informal survey which revealed that all of the adolescents in our hospital at that particular time came from broken homes. Typical of these teens was John, a sixteen-year-old who entered the hospital under a load of discouragement. John's parents had separated following years of ferocious arguing and fighting, and John was shuffled back and forth between mom and dad. John's parents continued their vicious battles over the custody of their children, while John and his siblings bounced from one parent to another. Being deprived of a complete family unit created more heartbreak than John could bear. His severe depression accompanied by serious efforts to harm himself were clearly an outgrowth of his having been ripped apart by family pressures.

Did you ever hear anyone say, "Divorce causes more problems than it resolves"? Only families who have experienced divorce or separation know how true this statement really is.

My experience in counseling causes me to proclaim with everything in me that every couple should receive counseling before things get to the point of separation or divorce. Sound Christian counseling can go a long way to alleviate or minimize the turmoil and stress accompanying family breakdown.

Stage three—The one-parent family
Following a divorce or separation, the family generally goes through a stage where one

parent, usually mother, is in charge of the family. This type of family structure can be illustrated in the following manner:

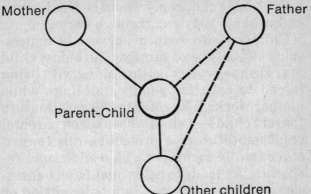

Mother

Father

Parent-Child

Other children

Many women who are desperately trying to hold their families together without the support of husbands or fathers suffer from depression. Pressing demands of working, of trying to be both mother and father, of child discipline, and of home management take their toll on women who are forced to manage their families alone. Such women frequently resent their ex-husbands who seem to have gotten out of the marriage scot-free while the wives are left holding the bag. While the ex-husband is at liberty to date other women, the wife may have almost no social life. His earnings may continue to grow, but she may receive a mere pittance and can barely meet her bills on a meager salary. Her resentment may be internalized into depression or projected onto the children. Thoughts such as "If I didn't have children, I would be free like my ex-husband" may run through her mind.

Children also reap a harvest of depression in this type of family. The oldest child may rush to protect mother along with being forced to care for younger siblings while mother works. (We refer to this position as a "parent child"—a child who takes on parental responsibilities or a protective role toward other family members.) This additional responsibility leads to resentment and depression as a teen is forced into baby-sitting or child care, while friends are having fun with their peers.

Young men in this type of family are frequently told, "You have to be the man of the house now that your father is gone." Being the "man of the house" is a pressure-packed role for a teen-ager who is seeking to put his own identity together.

Young women are frequently denied adequate male attention in a one-parent family. Girls who are deprived of a father's affection may end up in unfortunate relationships with boys or older men, leaving them discouraged and disillusioned about heterosexual relationships.

Mrs. Shirley Jones, a tired-looking, pale, emaciated Christian woman in her early thirties, brought her family in for counseling. The first interview with Shirley revealed many of the problems mentioned in this description of one-parent families. Mr. Jones left his wife when their two children were young, and Shirley desperately sought affection in other quarters. After bouncing off relationships with several men, Mrs. Jones decided to give them the boot and raise her children alone. However, Shirley's family had grown rapidly from two to seven children. This made the going rough for Shirley, who possessed an extremely poor self-image and a king-sized depression by the time she reached me. Shirley resented the men in her life, because "they had their fun, then ran off letting me hold the bag. They're earning high salaries, but I only receive social security benefits and can hardly make ends meet. The men who dumped me won't lift a finger to help me or visit their children."

Shirley eventually became overwhelmed with the demands of raising a large family without the support of a husband. Her little ones freely talked back, while teen-agers were openly rebellious. "I'm not going to listen to mother, I'm just going to do my own thing," Shirley's teen-age son told me in a private counseling session.

Counseling a one-parent family like Shirley's is difficult and time consuming. The best efforts of a counselor, as well as the support of other Christians, are generally required to make inroads into such difficult situations. Tangled interpersonal relationships which take years to develop do not unravel overnight. My approach called for giving Shirley massive doses of support as an adequate woman and mother. I encouraged her to take a more active disciplinary role by setting limits and sticking to them. We invited mature men and women in Shirley's church to be big brothers and sisters to her children. Shirley's pastor and his wife were included to assist their parishioner in managing a most difficult home situation. Combined efforts of church and counselor bore fruit as Shirley grew in her walk with the Lord and took a firmer hand in family affairs.

Stage four—The semi-blended family

In this stage the mother takes on a boyfriend who begins to assume some authority in the family. Very often the boyfriend moves in with the family before any marriage vows are spoken. The family can now be diagramed in this manner:

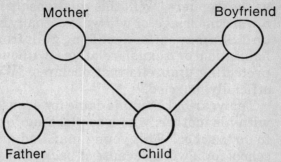

The situation worsens, especially for children who are caught up in this type of situation. There is a substitute father to relate to but what is his role? How much authority does he have, and what are his legal rights? He is generally viewed as an intruder by the children, for boyfriends can never replace fathers. Children are perplexed as to how to relate to mom's boyfriend, and even how to address him can be a dilemma (should they refer to him as dad, stepfather, or by his first name?). Furthermore, father is still in the picture, visiting regularly and pulling at the children's heartstrings. What a depressing picture this presents for children caught in this predicament.

This situation may also be less than pleasant for a woman. She may find herself pulled between conflicting demands of boyfriend and children. Insecurity may bog her down as she wonders, "Will this relationship move toward marriage, or will we eventually break up?" She may suffer agonizing guilt from cohabitation or sexual relations without the protecting umbrella that declares, "We are officially married."

Ten-year-old Tommie came for counseling with his mother, who was pleading for him to go to school. This young man had missed school for a week because of back pain and a headache. Tom's doctor gave him a clean bill of health and referred the family to me for counseling. Exploring the family situation revealed that mother's boyfriend had moved into the home one month ago. "Mom's boyfriend really throws his weight around; he wants to make us kids into his image of a perfect child," Tommie said in describing his family situation.

An interview with Tom's family revealed that mother's boyfriend, Andrew, was bent on shaping this family into his own image. "These kids have never been disciplined—they walk all over their mother. It's time someone made them behave," Andrew declared as he assessed the family situation.

Tommie protested the drastic changes occurring at home by silently developing physical symptoms primarily induced by emotional causes. His siblings were more vocal, as they echoed their strong feelings that Andrew instituted changes far too rapidly for them to cope with.

A close look at this family situation revealed that Tom's mother, Marie, was also becoming increasingly upset and depressed. She was caught in an impossible double bind with her boyfriend, who was demanding, "Make these children mind," and her children, who were pleading, "Mother, you've simply got to stop Andrew from putting all this pressure on us." She was the mediator between Andrew and the children, as both parties came to her with complaints. This turbulent situation resulted in an acute depression as Marie was caught directly in the crossfire between two conflicting forces.

Semi-blended families bring numerous challenges which test the skill of a family counselor. I worked closely with Andrew to help him ease up on the children until he could build a bridge of acceptance and love to them. I also helped Marie's children respect Andrew, pointing out that he was a figure in the home who had to be reckoned with. However, the most significant intervention was encouraging Andrew and the children direct access to each other, rather than communicating through Marie. This allowed Andrew to develop a more positive relationship with the children, and took Marie out of the cross-fire of conflicting demands from warring forces within the family. These interventions resulted in easing the stress and strain which was causing depression for several members of this family.

Stage five—The blended family

This stage also brings many perplexities as divorced parents from previous marriages unite their forces in a new family. Children from the prior marriages of both parents are brought into the family constellation, and the couple frequently give birth to their own children. This results in an interesting family constellation I refer to as "My kids, your kids, and our kids." The family structure now looks like this:

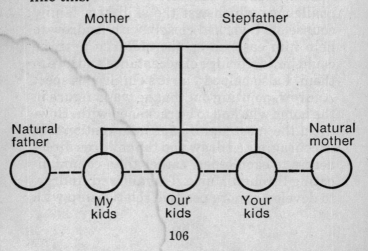

This family constellation occurs at an alarming rate in our society as divorce and remarriage become more common and increasingly acceptable. Possibilities for depression arise on every hand as family members struggle to make crucial adjustments. Parents face the gigantic task of attempting to relate to another spouse who brings a new set of children into the home. Sibling relationships become strained as bedrooms, personal belongings, finances, and other scarce family resources must be shared. Sibling rivalry is rampant as the children vie for parental recognition and approval. "My kids" watch "your kids," who in turn observe "our kids" to make sure that favoritism doesn't develop for one group over the other.

Pressures sometimes become so unbearable that children are shipped off to live with their other parent. A devastating situation results as children are bounced like a Ping-Pong ball from one parent to another, constantly being called upon to adapt to new situations.

One of the most heartbreaking scenes one can possibly imagine is a court hearing that features ex-spouses battling for their children's custody. Skeletons from the past tumble out of the closet as each parent sadistically tries to prove the other unfit. Children are torn apart, overwhelmed with love and loyalty for each parent. Children may be required to testify, forcing an expression of greater devotion to one parent than to the other. The uncertainty of a cloudy future hangs heavily over these children, who are overwhelmed with perplexing questions such as "Where will we be living next week?" or "I wonder what tomorrow holds for me?"

The Roberts family came for counseling with their eight children, three from each of Mr. and Mrs. Roberts' previous marriages, and two of their own. Mr. and Mrs. Roberts found solace in their relationship with each other as they bounced off troublesome marriages right into each other's arms. They discovered many common interests and were deeply in love with each other. They rushed headlong into marriage, scarcely recognizing the potential pitfalls of bringing two families together.

The Roberts family quickly fell into many of the patterns described in this section. The children fought ferociously with each other and manipulated their parents for special privileges and favors. Ten people were packed into a three-bedroom home, requiring several children to share bedroom space designed for one or two individuals. Much to their surprise, Mr. and Mrs. Roberts found themselves expressing greater loyalty to their own off-spring. Attempting to bring two sets of siblings together was a nightmare that became even more complicated when the union of Mr. and Mrs. Roberts produced additional children.

The tangled interpersonal relationships of a blended family represent the most difficult family constellation I counsel with. Frankly, I have very little success in attempting to bring harmony into families with complex relationships such as these. The intensely intricate blend of stepparents, natural parents, and several sets of siblings make this family environment a hotbed of potential emotional problems. The best advice I can give is: Don't allow yourself to get caught up in this type of family situation.

Your Attitude Is the Key

Perhaps you have origins in less than ideal family circumstances. Does this mean you are predestined to have emotional problems or that nothing can be done to head off depression? A thousand times no! A troubled family environment does not guarantee a life full of problems any more than positive family interaction promises a carefree existence.

If you grew up in a family like one of those

described in this chapter, your attitude steers you toward, or away from, depression. Here are some common reactions toward troubled family life which bog people down with depression.

Self-pity

"Why did I have such a bad family? I wouldn't have so many problems if it wasn't for my rotten home life."

Some people insist on feeling sorry for themselves because they have never experienced satisfying family relationships. They are like Theresa, a young woman in her twenties who grew up with conflict and tension in her home. Theresa's parents fought ferociously with each other throughout her formative years. Theresa said, "I cried myself to sleep many nights listening to mother and father argue." Sadness and dejection carried into adulthood as obsessive thoughts about her less than ideal family mired Theresa in self-pity. Theresa came to a screeching halt as she rejected her housework responsibilities, completely pushing child care onto her husband.

When I confronted Theresa with her responsibilities as a wife and mother, she responded in a "yes, but" manner by saying, "Yes, but you don't understand what it was

110

like to grow up in a family where there was conflict and tension. I know I need to care for my husband and children, but I can't get over not having a good family when I was young." Theresa wrapped herself tightly in a blanket of self-pity as she became mired down in discouragement over a family life that had been characterized by division and strife.

Rigidity and inflexibility

"I can't change because of my troubled family situation."

Some people convince themselves and others that their family backgrounds lock them into deep, inescapable ruts. They declare that their troubled family upbringing dooms them to a load of despair and difficulty. This good news for individuals tied into such thinking patterns needs to be declared loudly and clearly: Thousands of individuals manage well in spite of a less than ideal family environment. People can rise above circumstances which seem to lock them into discouraging living patterns. Here are some quotes from a study I conducted on healthy Christian families which indicate hope for individuals from troubled backgrounds.

"My family life was not good in that my parents didn't express their feelings. I am trying to express myself much more fully than my parents did."

"Because my parents had a troubled marriage, I am working extra hard to make mine a good one."

"I am trying to be a warm, loving parent to my children, because I realize how much I missed love from my parents."

"Because of lack of communication and affection between my parents, I have deliberately sought for both of these in my own marriage."

"My parents argued a lot. This made me feel insecure. However, it made me want to grow personally and have a better marriage than they had."

You see, it is possible to grow beyond the example presented to you by your family as you grew up.

Projecting blame

"It's my family's fault that I am depressed."

Listen to a discouraged individual's conversation to see if you can spot attitudes such as the following:

"If it wasn't for the partner God gave me, I wouldn't get so discouraged."

"My parents messed my life up. I get discouraged every time I remember the way they treated me."

"I can't help but feel depressed. It all comes from my bad family life."

Blaming other people for our problems is a defensive cop-out. A far more realistic approach is to take responsibility for one's own behavior, coping as constructively as possible with life's troublesome situations.

Resentment and unforgiveness

"I can never forgive my parents for the way they treated me."

Intense resentment, bitter condemnation, and stubborn unforgiveness toward family members can result in severe emotional hang-ups. Conversely, gracious acceptance, heartfelt forgiveness, and loving patience takes people a long way down the road toward emotional wholeness.

My wife grew up in a divided home where she could have developed the negative attitudes mentioned above. However, in spite of less than ideal circumstances, she never grumbles or complains about her family. She does not allow herself to become bogged down in self-pity or to blame her family for the problems she encounters. This wholesome attitude, I am convinced, is a key to the positive adjustment she enjoys as an emotionally healthy woman.

Biblical Personalities, Family Pressures, and Depression

Can you imagine losing all your children at once? Job's children were snuffed out by a mighty windstorm, leaving only Job and his wife to comfort each other. This type of situation should push a husband and wife into each other's arms, clinging to each other for mutual support. However, Job's wife could hardly tolerate a painful look at her agonizingly pitiful husband. She added insult to injury as she blurted out, "Are you still trying to be godly when God has done all this to you? Curse him and die" (Job 2:9). How devastating to be rejected by the person closest to you in your hour of greatest need.

David was another individual who encountered marital and family stress on every hand. King David's wife, Michal, pounced on him with an extremely critical attitude. She referred to her husband as vain and disgusting following an occasion when David danced before the Lord. When the ark of the covenant had returned home, "David returned to bless his family. But Michal came out to meet

him in disgust. 'How glorious the king of
Israel looked today! He exposed himself to
the girls along the street like a common per-
vert!' David retorted, 'I was dancing before
the Lord who chose me above your father and
his family and who appointed me as leader
of Israel, the people of the Lord' " (2 Sam.
6:20-23).

One cannot help but wonder if Michal's ac-
cusing and critical attitude was not a factor
in pushing David into the arms of a statu-
esque woman named Bathsheba.

Marital stress and unfaithfulness always
take a terrible toll on the children. King
David's rebellious son Absalom stabbed dad
in the back, trying with all his strength to
wrench the kingdom from his father's hands.
However, Absalom's threat to the kingdom
ended abruptly as he was assassinated while
entrapped in the sturdy limbs of a giant oak
tree. Absalom's death seemed to be a cause
for rejoicing, for a major threat to David's
kingdom had suddenly disappeared. Hear
David's pathetic cry, revealing anguish, sorrow, and pathos, as he confronts the death of
his wayward son: "O my son Absalom, my
son, my son, Absalom! would God I had died
for thee, O Absalom, my son, my son!" (2 Sam.
18:33, KJV).

"My son, my son." This pathetic cry for a

prodigal son is multiplied thousands of times today. The pitiful cries of spouses who are separating and children without complete family units are equally agonizing. This chapter clearly demonstrates that all members are candidates for depression when family deterioration sets in.

However, there is another side to this coin. The well-functioning Christian family is the greatest bulwark against depression and other emotional problems that exists in our society. A healthy family reduces the potential for anger, self-pity, and relationship problems from which depression springs. You are giving your family a wellspring of pure, fresh water that will nourish and enhance the mental health of each member as you build a solid Christian home.

8

The Heavens Are As Brass

We cannot adequately assess the causes of depression without discussing the role of sin as a contributing factor. Wrongdoing as an element in depression becomes crystal clear as I ponder the circumstances surrounding clients who knock on my door for help with discouragement. For instance, a young depressed housewife recently confessed that she was haunted by guilt and remorse over a number of premarital and extramarital sexual escapades. A prominent member of a nearby church became bogged down with deep depression after she was apprehended for shoplifting. Another high-ranking church official was haunted by depression after being nabbed for propositioning a young lady. My caseload consists of depressed homosexuals, men and women actively engaged in adultery, people who smoke pot or take other street drugs—and all of these people are professing Christians.

It may surprise you to realize that Christians could fall into such wrong behavior. Many people believe Christians have lily-white hands, and they spend their lives piously going about doing good, rarely breaking God's commandments. Working as a counselor provides shocking revelations regarding the deep sins Christians can fall into.

The Bible emphatically affirms that wrong behavior is always accompanied by a payday. "For the wages of sin is death," declares God's Word (Rom. 6:23). "Depression" may be stamped indelibly on your pay stub as a consequence of sinful behavior.

Wrongdoing leads to conflict, a root cause of depression. Christians have a built-in sense of right and wrong which springs forth from biblical teaching. Going against what you have been taught automatically triggers a still small voice within that says, "This is against everything you know to be correct behavior."

The Bible boldly declares that "The soul that sinneth, it shall die" (Ezek. 18:4, KJV). Deliberately disobeying God's laws will generally not result in immediate physical death. However, depression may be one form of inner death that springs from sinful behavior. Depressed people often confess to a death of the inner person—it is almost as if their very souls, the seats of their emotions, have evaporated. People who traverse valleys of deep depression realize this may be the most painful and difficult of all deaths.

David is a classical example of a biblical personality who experienced depression following wrongdoing. Many of David's discouraging moments could be traced directly to his adulterous relationship with Bathsheba and the intrigue and murder in its wake. Gripped with guilt and remorse, David cried to the Lord:

Have mercy upon me, O God, according to thy lovingkindness: according unto the multitude of thy tender mercies blot out my transgressions. Wash me throughly from mine iniquity, and cleanse me from my sin. For I acknowledge my transgressions: and my sin is ever before me. Against thee, thee only, have I sinned, and done this evil in thy sight: that thou mightest be justified when thou speakest, and be clear when thou judgest. Behold, I was shapen in iniquity; and in sin did my mother conceive me. Behold, thou desirest truth in the inward parts: and in the hidden part thou shalt make me to know wisdom. Purge me with hyssop, and I shall be clean: wash me, and I shall be whiter than snow. Make me to hear joy and gladness; that the bones which thou hast broken may rejoice. Hide thy face from my sins, and blot out all mine iniquities. Create in me a clean heart, O God; and renew a right spirit within me. Cast me not away from thy presence; and take not thy holy spirit from me. Restore unto me the joy of thy salvation; and uphold me with thy free spirit. (Ps. 51:1-12, KJV)

A gospel message which squarely confronts the reality of sin is a powerful deterrent to depression. Believers and nonbelievers need to be warned of the dreadful emotional consequences of sinful behavior. Unfortunately, much of Christendom heartily embraces psychological causes of human behavior, denying wrongdoing as a causative factor. Ministers should develop their counseling skills, but clergymen should not substitute counseling and psychological principles in place of the Word of God. Interestingly enough, psychologists and psychiatrists are beginning to focus attention on sin as a root cause of mental illness—a fascinating reversal, indeed.

Dr. Karl Menninger, one of America's foremost psychiatrists, has authored a provocative book entitled, *Whatever Became of Sin?* This book is a fervent plea to sharpen our individual and collective consciences regarding sin. Menninger contends that this is everyone's role, but he especially challenges the clergy to spearhead efforts that will call our nation back to a sin consciousness:

> If the moribund term "sin" with its full implications is ever revived, we will all have to have a voice in it. But the clergy will have reasserted an authority from leadership in the moral field which they have let slip from their hands. It is their special prerogative to study sin—or whatever they call it—to identify it, to define it, to warn us about it, and to spur measures for combating and rectifying it. Have they been diverted or discouraged from their task? Have they succumbed to the feeling that law and science and technology have proved morality and moral leadership irrelevant? Did they, too, fall for the illusion that sin had really vanished?[1]

> The clergyman cannot minimize sin and maintain his proper role in our culture. If he, or we ourselves, "say we have no sin, we deceive ourselves, and the truth is not in us" (1 John 1:8). We need him as our umpire to direct us, to accuse us, to reproach us, to exhort us, to intercede for us, to shrive us. Failure to do so is his sin.[2]

---

[1]Karl Menninger, *Whatever Became of Sin?*, (New York: Hawthorn Books, 1973), p. 192.
[2]Ibid., p. 198.

We can readily visualize a scathing attack on sin from a pulpit-pounding, arm-waving, foot-stomping evangelist or preacher. However, this same expectation does not hold true for a gentleman who is schooled in the medical arts. Nevertheless, it is a distinguished psychiatrist who makes this declaration about sin:

> In all of the laments and reproaches made by our seers and prophets, one misses any mention of "sin," a word which used to be a veritable watchword of prophets. It was a word once in everyone's mind, but now rarely if ever heard. Does this mean that no sin is involved in all our troubles—sin with an "I" in the middle? Is no one any longer guilty of anything? Guilty perhaps of a sin that could be repented and repaired or atoned for? Is it only that someone may be stupid or sick or criminal—or asleep? Wrong things are being done, we know; tares are being sown in the wheat field at night. But is no one responsible, no one answerable for these acts? Anxiety and depression we all acknowledge, and even vague guilt feelings; but has no one committed any sins?[3]

The very word "sin," which seems to have disappeared, was a proud word. It was once a

---

[3]Ibid., p. 13.

strong word, an ominous and serious word. It described a central point in every civilized human being's life plan and life style. But the word went away. It has almost disappeared— the word along with the notion. Why? Doesn't anyone sin anymore? Doesn't anyone believe in sin?[4]

Menninger asserts that the word "sin" began to disappear from our national vocabulary approximately twenty years ago. He further declares that behavior which should be labeled "sinful" is neatly wrapped up in euphemistic packages carrying labels such as sickness, emotional problems, psychological disorders, legal offenses, behavior problems, etc.

Identifying sin as one of the root causes of emotional disorders supplies an important link in the chain of healing. However, a solution to the sin problem must be discovered before the patient can be pronounced "cured."

Everyone can rejoice because there is a positive remedy for depression caused by sinful behavior. Heartfelt confession and repentance which results in turning one's back on wrong behavior is the key. The same Scripture that declares, "The wages of sin is death," also contains an effective cure for the

---

[4]Ibid., p. 14.

problem: "The gift of God is eternal life through Jesus Christ our Lord" (Rom. 6:23, KJV).

The Bible further stipulates a remedy for wrong behavior along with the potential for healing in a passage addressed to believers: "If my people, which are called by my name, shall humble themselves, and pray, and seek my face, and turn from their wicked ways; then will I hear from heaven, and will forgive their sin, and will heal their land" (2 Chron. 7:14, KJV).

Coming down from the mountain

Sometimes depression follows a spiritual victory or a mountaintop experience. A trek up the mountain is usually followed by a journey into the valley. The discouraging real world may hit us like a freight train following an uplifting spiritual experience.

As we have seen, Elijah teamed up with God to win a miraculous victory over Baal's false prophets. This great victory over the forces of evil was a triumphal occasion that should have brought forth rejoicing. However, soon after this experience, a depressed Elijah sits under a bush begging the Lord to take his life.

My work as a counselor opens up numerous doors to minister to Christians in various settings. I often find myself becoming discouraged following a meeting where the Lord has blessed in a special way. I am aware that Satan's attack is intensified after a spiritual victory. His daggers following a mountaintop experience may bog us down in depression.

It is also possible to experience depression following a spiritual defeat. Peter's denial of the Lord illustrates this, as Peter went out and wept sorrowfully following this experience (Luke 22:62). Peter's bitter tears represented more than sadness. Peter undoubtedly convulsed with remorse, anguish, and depression from the depths of his heart.

Like Peter, we could fix our gaze on our spiritual failures and become depressed. Satan uses times when we are down spiritually to push us toward greater discouragement. However, the Lord forgave and reclaimed Peter following his denial. Likewise, He is there to forgive and restore you when you stumble in your Christian experience. He is just waiting to welcome you back to the fold.

9

How Can I Recognize Depression?

Surprisingly, many individuals who seek counseling simply do not realize they are depressed. They are firmly convinced that something is dreadfully wrong with their bodies or minds. Depressed people commonly remark, "I feel like I am losing my mind," or "I'm beginning to believe I am cracking up." Others, convinced that they are physically ill, run from one doctor to another seeking relief for their problems. Such individuals are frequently astonished to discover that they are depressed, and that the prognosis for their recovery is most hopeful.

In addition, individuals who come in contact with deeply discouraged people miss the telltale signs of depression. Depression readily hides behind a mask of defenses, marital problems, or somatic complaints. Looking beyond exterior symptoms and cutting directly to the heart of the problem frequently reveals a person suffering from acute depression.

Familiarizing ourselves with the warning signs of depression allows us to deal more effectively with discouragement in ourselves and others. Depression is generally characterized by a particular cluster of symptoms or manifestations which allows a fairly clear and precise diagnosis. Therefore, this chapter seeks to enhance our understanding of depression by describing symptoms generally found in deeply discouraged individuals.

1. *Profound changes in eating patterns—"My appetite is gone"*

Depressed people almost always experience drastic alterations in their eating habits. One of the first inquiries I make when evaluating someone for depression is "How is your appetite?"

Changes in eating patterns can manifest themselves in various ways during depression. Sometimes an individual's desire for food increases when he is depressed. People may shovel great amounts of food into their systems in an effort to ward off discouragement. Food becomes a security blanket that compensates for loneliness and discouragement. Unfortunately, the weight gain that results from overeating may lead to a negative self-concept which, in turn, reinforces depression.

However, a person's appetite generally takes a nose dive when he becomes deeply discouraged. People going through depression make statements such as, "I just don't feel like eating; food is tasteless and it sticks to the roof of my mouth; I gag at the thought of eating."

Sometimes depressed people will lose weight rather rapidly. For instance, a discouraged individual I once worked with lost over fifty pounds as her weight dropped from 140 to less than 90. This kind of weight loss can be extremely dangerous. Therefore, I wouldn't suggest getting depressed as a means for losing weight.

Job's appetite almost totally disappeared when he was depressed. Job said, "I cannot eat for sighing " (3:24). Job looked at an egg and stated, "My appetite is gone when I look at it. I gag at the thought of eating it" (6:7). David also had a problem with his appetite when he was depressed. During a time of discouragement David said, "My food is tasteless, and I have lost my appetite" (Ps. 102:4).

2. *Changes in sleep patterns—"I toss and turn all night"*

The second question I ask someone who is

depressed is "Are you sleeping satisfactorily?" Depressed people often report drastic changes in their normal sleeping behavior. A depressed person who is plagued by insomnia may lay awake for hours. His inability to relax may cause him to pace the floor in an effort to relieve agitation.

Some depressed people fall asleep shortly after retiring, but awaken soon thereafter. The ticking clock resounds like a jackhammer as they stare into the darkness. These individuals are alert to people stirring around the neighborhood in the wee hours of the night. In counseling sessions, it is common for depressed people to report that they haven't slept well for several months.

Job was haunted by sleep disturbances and bad dreams. Can you imagine trying to sleep when your body is covered by boils? This was Job's predicament as he cried out, "even when I try to forget my misery in sleep, you terrify with nightmares" (7:14). Job spoke of long, weary nights, "When I go to bed I think, 'Oh, that it were morning,' and then I toss till dawn" (7:4).

Did you ever have a sleepless night when it seemed your night clothes continuously wrapped around you? This was Job's situation when he said: "Depression haunts my days. My weary nights are filled with pain as though something were relentlessly gnawing at my bones. All night long I toss and turn, and my garments bind about me" (30:16-18).

3. *Retreating to the bed—"All I want to do is lay around"*

Retreating to the couch or bed as a refuge is commonly seen in depression. Spending time in bed when there is work to do is a retreat from reality and an escape from responsibility. A discouraged housewife tells of guilt feelings precipitated by laying around on the couch all day. She states, "I know I am neglecting my family, but I just don't have the drive to do anything." A depressed man who has been a steady worker reports he no longer has the motivation to pull himself out of bed to get to work. Responsibility flies out the window as depressed people shrink from the demands of life, escaping into the cocoon they spin around themselves in bed.

A couple brought their young adult daughter for counseling, stating that she had been retreating to her bed for the past month. These parents described their problem in this way: "The situation with our daughter Jean is that her movement is practically restricted to a trip from the bed to the couch. It seems that she wants to sleep until noon, then spends the afternoon laying around. We are at our wits end to know how to motivate her. Can you help us to find a way to encourage our daughter to function again?"

Talking with Jean revealed she was utilizing the bed as an escape from responsibilities that terrified her. Jean required hospital care and intensive counseling to overcome depression and resume responsibilities once again.

Job also found comfort and solace in his bed. "My bed shall comfort me, my couch shall ease my complaint," he said (7:13, KJV).

4. Isolating oneself from other people—"No one cares about me"

Depressed people may feel that no one cares about them or that other people are looking down on them. They sometimes bar themselves inside their houses because they view the outside world as hostile and unfriendly.

A depressed lady named Alice believed the whole neighborhood was talking about her. "None of my neighbors like me, they're all down on me," Alice told me in a counseling session. This lonely lady isolated herself in her home for days, hardly bothering to talk to anyone. Very much a loner, Alice didn't have any friends and felt rejected by the people around her.

Job also felt forsaken by his friends and

neighbors. He believed the whole town was talking about him and poking fun at him because of his predicament. "I, the man who begged God for help, and God answered him, have become a laughingstock to my neighbors. Yes, I, a righteous man, am now the man they scoff at" (12:4).

Although David ordinarily had a positive attitude toward people, he also believed that people were mocking him when he was discouraged. "But I am a worm, not a man, scorned and despised by my own people and by all mankind. Everyone who sees me mocks and sneers and shrugs. 'Is this the one who rolled his burden on the Lord?' they laugh. 'Is this the one who claims the Lord delights in him? We'll believe it when we see God rescue him" (Ps. 22:6-8).

5. *Feeling blocked off from the Lord—"God seems a million miles away"*

Christians who are depressed usually feel thwarted from reaching out to the Lord. Depression seems to build a wall between a Christian and his Lord, and God seems a million miles away. Depressed people believe God has gone on an extended vacation and has forgotten about them.

John was a young Christian man who came for a counseling session with slumped shoulders and a drooped appearance. John moved at a snail's pace as we walked together to my office. This distressed man's depression manifested itself primarily in spiritual struggles. John believed his faith was nonexistent, and stated, "Jesus said we can do anything with faith as large as a mustard seed. My faith isn't that big; in fact, I don't have any faith at all." John felt blocked off from the Lord, and he told me, "I just can't get through to God. I pray as hard as I can, but my prayers don't seem to get beyond the ceiling." John was basically a fine Christian, but his spiritual growth was stunted because of the depression he was experiencing.

Depressed Christians like John often believe they have a spiritual problem when they are locked in the depths of discouragement. It is common for Christians to state that they are "spiritually bankrupt," "totally backslidden," or "spiritually depraved" when they are depressed. Some people believe they have committed the unpardonable sin because they can't make contact with God. However, while spiritual conflicts may be one cause of depression, discouragement does not necessarily indicate a break in our relationship with God. Emotional problems such as depression can build a wall that temporarily blocks us off from the Lord.

Job could identify very closely with a discouraged Christian who feels blocked off from the Lord. Job cried out, "Oh, how I long to speak directly to the Almighty. I want to talk this over with God himself" (13:3). "Oh, that I knew where to find God. . . . But I search in vain. I seek him here, I seek him there and cannot find him. . . . I seek him in his workshop in the North, but cannot find him there; nor can I find him in the South; there, too, he hides himself" (23:3, 8-9). Job felt like God was ignoring him and said: "I cry to you, O God, but you don't answer me. I stand before you and you don't bother to look" (30:20).

David also felt forsaken and punished by God. Although these prophetic words refer to Jesus, David was also expressing his own thoughts when he said, "My God, my God, why have you forsaken me? Why do you refuse to help me or even to listen to my groans? Day and night I keep on weeping, crying for your help, but there is no reply" (Ps. 22:1-2). David also expressed his feelings in this way: "Lord, how long will you stand there, doing nothing? Act now and rescue me, for I have but one life and these young lions are out to get it" (Ps. 35:17).

A depressed person may believe God is rejecting or condemning him. They see God as an ogre in the sky who is poised to pounce on them. "I am a terrible person and God is punishing me," a depressed person often says. Such feelings were very much in Job's thought patterns as he stated, "For I know that you will not hold me innocent, O God, but will condemn me. So what's the use of trying? . . . If I start to get up off the ground, you leap upon me like a lion and quickly finish me off" (Job 9:28-29; 10:16). "God hates me and angrily tears at my flesh" (Job 16:9).

Job felt harassed by God when he said, "What is mere man that you spend your time persecuting him? . . . Why have you made me your target, and made life so heavy a burden to me?" (Job 7:17, 20). "You give me so few steps upon the stage of life, and notice every mistake I make" (Job 14:16).

David talked to God in a similar manner. "O Lord, don't punish me while you are angry! Your arrows have struck deep; your blows are crushing me. Because of your anger my body is sick, my health is broken beneath my sins. They are like a flood, higher than my head; they are a burden too heavy to bear" (Ps. 38:1-4).

It is most gratifying to witness a Christian's relationship with the Lord dramatically improve as his depression vanishes. Patients who once said, "I cannot read my Bible or pray" will relish the delight of drinking at the fountain of God's joy as their depression lifts. Contact is reestablished with the Lord as a prayer channel miraculously opens up. The Bible is removed from the shelf and dusted off as the individual once again drinks from the wellspring of Scripture. A Christian who refuses to attend church services while depressed reestablishes vital worship patterns as discouragement disappears.

Diane was a deeply depressed young woman who couldn't pray or read her Bible. Her emotional problems prevented her from believing God was still on His throne. After several counseling sessions, Diane came in with a sparkle in her eye, carrying her Bible in her hand. She opened the Word and read several meaningful passages to me as tears trickled down her cheeks. I realized that Diane was moving out of her depressed state as the Word became meaningful to her once again.

6. *Dwelling in the past—"My good days are gone forever"*

People who are depressed tend to live in the past, constantly reminiscing about the "good ol' days." They commonly believe that their lives have ended and see no hope for the present or future.

A depressed young man named Ted was in bed when I first talked with him. I hit on a sensitive nerve in our conversation which made him sit up straight, shake his finger angrily at me and say, "Get out of here and leave me alone. I don't want your help and I don't want to get well. All my good days are in the past. I have no future and there's nothing for me to live for." Ted abruptly dismissed me and buried himself under a blanket from head to toe.

At the root of Ted's problem was a poor self-image. He believed he was a total failure, and could not see anything to build upon as he faced the future. Ted and I worked hard in subsequent counseling sessions to help him see his self-worth. Other staff in our hospital consistently pointed out Ted's value in God's sight. These fresh insights into the worth of his personhood slowly chipped away at Ted's negative self-image. As he saw himself in a more positive light, he was able to lay aside his preoccupation with the past and face the future with greater confidence.

Job had feelings similar to Ted's. "My good days are in the past," Job said (Job 17:11). He yearned for history to repeat itself, "Oh, for the years gone by when God took care of me. . . . when I went out to the city gate and took my place among the honored elders"

(Job 29:2, 7). He longed to return to the time when everyone respected and honored him. "All who saw me spoke well of me" (Job 29:11). Job recalled how people in the city sought his counsel: "Everyone listened to me and valued my advice, and were silent until I spoke. And after I spoke, they spoke no more, for my counsel satisfied them" (Job 29:21-22). In thinking about the past, Job recalled the days when he encouraged other depressed people. "When they were discouraged, I smiled and that encouraged them, and lightened their spirits" (Job 29:24).

David also thought of the past during times of discouragement. "Do you remember those times (but how could you ever forget them!) when you led a great procession to the Temple on festival days, singing with joy, praising the Lord?" (Ps. 42:4-5).

7. *Self-centeredness—"I am the center of my world"*

Self-centeredness and preoccupation with oneself often accompanies depression. Listen to a depressed person speak and notice how he is wrapped up in his own little world. These individuals wish to be the star of the show, always pushing to assume center stage in the drama of life.

This all-encompassing concern for oneself

often leads to worry about physical health. Consequently, physical complaints such as nausea, headaches, and back ailments may accompany depression. Depressed people sometimes believe they have a fatal illness. It is common for a counselor to hear statements such as, "I'm sure the doctor will discover I have diabetes; the old ticker isn't working like it used to; I would bet my bottom dollar that I have cancer; are you absolutely positive that there's nothing physically wrong with me?"

A lady named JoAnn had been to nearly a dozen doctors, who all told her she was in sound physical condition. Yet she suffered from headaches and dizziness, and sometimes she would nearly pass out. In spite of all the reassurance from her doctors, JoAnn continued to insist she was physically ill. "They just haven't found what's wrong with me yet" was JoAnn's attitude. "The next doctor I consult with will discover my problem."

JoAnn's persistent view that her health was bad resulted in colossal medical bills that threatened the family's financial well-being. Eventually one of her doctors helped JoAnn recognize that depression was her problem, and suggested that she seek counseling.

Underlying JoAnn's preoccupation with

her physical health was a strong drive for attention. Her husband, John, was a busy executive who spent little time at home. However, he would move into action very speedily whenever JoAnn threatened to pass out. Such episodes often culminated with John rushing his wife to a hospital emergency room where the message would always be, "There's absolutely nothing physically wrong with you!"

Counseling helped JoAnn understand her tendency to seek attention through depression and physical symptoms. At the same time, her husband became aware of how he could offer more love and support to his wife. Through intense marital therapy, this couple was able to learn new ways of satisfying each other's needs.

Job worried about his health in much the same way that JoAnn did. While looking at a reflection of himself, Job declared, "I am a shadow of my former self" (Job 17:7). He stated further, "I am black, but not from sunburn. . . . My skin is black and peeling. My bones burn with fever" (Job 30:28-30).

8. *Persistent despair and pessimism—"It's hopeless, why try any more?"*

A depressed person is filled with great despair and sees no hope for the present or future. Depressed people are ready to say "I give up" or "I quit." Because they feel life is no longer worth living, depressed people may consider self-destruction or make actual attempts to harm themselves.

The despair of deep discouragement makes depressed people feel like they are surrounded by impenetrable clouds of darkness. A depressed person feels as if he is walking through an endless black tunnel. To him, it appears that there is no ray of light whatsoever in the darkness.

A middle-aged fellow named Charlie reflected a totally hopeless attitude. "I just can't go on, there's no point in trying any more," Charlie said. "I feel like I am walking on and on in a dense fog. There's a thick blanket of heaviness following me wherever I go. I just can't seem to escape the darkness and break into the light again."

Job also experienced feelings of hopelessness and despair. He said, "For I am utterly helpless, without any hope" (Job 6:13). Further statements indicate his hopeless attitude as he said, "My hopes have disappeared. My heart's desires are broken. . . . Where then is my hope? Can anyone find any? No, my hope will go down with me to the grave. We shall rest together in the dust!" (Job 17:11, 15-16). Job's despair comes through as he looks at his life and states, "My life is but a breath, and nothing good is left" (Job 7:7).

The feeling of walking through an endless tunnel of fog and darkness also characterized Job's experience. He declared, "[There is] darkness all around me, thick, impenetrable darkness everywhere" (Job 23:17). "I waited for the light. Darkness came. My heart is troubled and restless. Waves of affliction have come upon me" (Job 30:26-27).

Job also believed life was not worth living and that he might as well die. Job's preoccupation with death comes through as he says, "I know that your purpose for me is death" (Job 30:23). "Oh, why should light and life be given to those in misery and bitterness, who long for death, and it won't come; who search for death as others search for food or money? What blessed relief when at last they die" (Job 3:20-22). "Oh, that God would grant me the thing I long for most—to die beneath his hand, and to be freed from his painful grip" (Job 6:8-9). Job displays his frustration with life by saying, "I am weary of living" (Job 10:1).

9. *Loss of interest—"I just don't feel like doing anything any more"*

A loss of interest in one's surroundings usually accompanies depression. Depressed people lose interest in their environment, so that the hobbies, interests, and goals they once pursued no longer have appeal. The avid fisherman puts his rod on the shelf. The whir of a seamstress's sewing machine is no longer heard.

Sexual interests and energies often vanish during depression. Statements such as, "I have no desire for sex" are commonly heard from depressed people. Individuals who are depressed may fear they are becoming impotent when they experience difficulty performing sexual activity. Problems relating to their spouses in this vital area of marriage often lead to embarrassment and guilt feelings regarding their inability to satisfy their spouses' needs.

A depressed person's family is usually troubled about their loved one's loss of interest in living. Husbands are puzzled when a wife no longer cooks and cleans the house with the vigor she once displayed. A family member reports, "Dad used to love to hunt and fish, but we can't get him to do any of these activities any more." A spouse feels rejected when a depressed partner no longer is interested in engaging in marital relations.

Each one of the depressed people mentioned in Scripture lost interest in their environments. Job, sitting on an ash heap for days, accomplished nothing. Elijah fled into the wilderness, and when the Lord spoke to him, he replied, in essence, "Leave me alone, I don't feel like doing anything" (1 Kings 19). Jonah, slumped under a bush in despair, lost all interest in his surroundings during a time of discouragement (Jonah 4).

10. *Molehills turn into mountains—"I just can't make decisions any more"*

Routine decisions once taken in stride assume the importance of a summit conference to a depressed individual. A small job seems like a hard day's work. A depressed person is a mass of mixed feelings, and has difficulty making up his mind about life's decisions.

Donna was a depressed lady who talked about decisions she faced with anyone who would lend an ear. Unable to make up her mind about life's pressing issues, Donna ran from person to person asking, "What do you think I should do about this problem?" Donna received conflicting advice from people, which soon resulted in severe confusion. Her inner turmoil about which way to turn caused Donna to withdraw from a world she believed it was impossible to live in.

We can hypothesize that Jonah must have experienced a bundle of mixed emotions regarding the work God called him to do. A part of Jonah probably told him to obey the Lord and go to Nineveh. Yet, an opposing force said, "Run away from what God wants you to do." Jonah tried to quiet these conflicting forces inside of him by hiding in a ship bound for Tarshish.

It is also reasonable to assume that Jonah was filled with conflict regarding his message to the corrupt residents of Nineveh. On the one hand, it must have been gratifying to witness this depraved city repent and turn from wickedness. However, a voice inside of Jonah probably said, "God promised that He would destroy this city, and He had jolly well better keep His word." Such opposing forces warring within Jonah's bosom surely must have contributed to his discouragement.

Summary

Understanding how depression manifests itself is extremely valuable in recognizing this problem in ourselves or others. Of course, an individual need not experience all the symptoms mentioned to be depressed. Deep discouragement will manifest itself uniquely in each particular individual. Some people may exhibit several of these symptoms, while others may display only one or two symptoms.

Here is a list of the ten major symptoms of

depression described in this chapter, for the purpose of review and easy reference.

1. Changes in appetite
2. Difficulty in sleeping
3. Shunning responsibility, retreating to the bed or couch
4. Believing no one cares
5. Feeling it is impossible to reach God
6. Living in the past
7. Self-centeredness
8. Loss of hope, believing there is nothing to live for
9. Losing interest in one's surroundings
10. Difficulty making decisions

Recognizing symptoms and understanding root causes are vital steps in our study of depression. The next big task is putting this information to work by helping ourselves or others about us who are discouraged. The following chapter will pay attention to this subject, as we identify methods of treating and overcoming depression.

How to Overcome the Blues and the Blahs

A perplexing network of agencies and programs confront a depressed person who is seeking help. Therefore, it is easy to become confused about which way to turn for services when depression strikes. "Where can I find the best treatment for the distress I am experiencing?" discouraged people may ask. "Could my doctor help me overcome this horrible problem, or would my minister provide a better resource? Is it right to take nerve medicine, or should I rely on the Lord? Is counseling appropriate, or is it best to battle these problems on my own?"

This chapter endeavors to diminish the confusion represented by these perplexing questions. Efforts to reach this goal are accomplished by examining up-to-date approaches to treating depression from the medical, psychological, recreational, and spiritual points of view.

Medical approaches in treating depression

A debate rages in the mental health field regarding organic or biochemical causes of depression versus emotional and familial factors. However, a particular type of depression, manic-depressive illness, seems to have a well-established biochemical root cause. Manic-depressive problems are characterized by rapid mood swings as individuals vacillate from periods of frenzied animation to the throes of depression. A person in a manic state is characterized by hyperactivity—he requires little sleep and seems tireless in his activities. Such individuals may go on spending sprees, write endless pages of material, or begin several projects at once. When they burn out, however, they sink low into the depths of discouragement.

A particular chemical, lithium carbonate, has proven to be an effective stabilizer for individuals with the symptoms described above. Lithium should be carefully administered and monitored by a physician, who orders blood tests to maintain the correct amount of this chemical in the system.

Medication can also be an effective adjunctive to counseling for depressions with an emotional or environmental base. Tranquilizers and antidepressants elevate a person's mood or calm anxiety and tension which accompany depression. Like lithium, these medications should also be taken under the careful prescription and direction of a physician who can regulate dosages and explain the side effects that chemicals may induce.

People frequently see medication as a cure-all for depression. While medication may effectively relieve symptoms and help a person function better, chemical treatment totally ignores psychological and spiritual root causes of depression. Therefore, a deeply discouraged individual should obtain counseling so that underlying problems can be unearthed and dealt with.

Our drug-oriented society makes it easy to assume that medication cures every ill known to man. A lady named Fanny came for counseling, and she stated, "I have been taking tranquilizers for my mental condition for twenty years." Consuming pills was a daily ritual for Fanny, who had been on every tranquilizer in the book. Her husband added, "I do not believe Fanny could function without drugs in her system. However, I am convinced it is only a matter of time until someone discovers or prescribes exactly the right combination of chemicals to cure my wife's problem."

Should Christians become dependent on medication to relieve anxiety and depression?

While medication can be useful for temporary relief of depressive symptoms, long-term dependence is unhealthy. Dependence on medication makes it easy for a person to topple when the crutch is removed. It is far better to deal with root causes of emotional problems than to constantly lean on medication to relieve symptoms.

Electric shock treatment is another medical device utilized to help depressed people. Electric shock treatment allows an electrical current to pass through a patient's body, resulting in a convulsion. While no one knows for sure why electric shock treatment helps people who are depressed, very dramatic recoveries from depression have been documented from this treatment. This once-popular antidote for depression is rapidly being replaced by medication and counseling. However, electric shock treatment may prove to be a useful device to relieve depression when other techniques have not been successful, or when rapid relief of depressive symptoms is called for. It is important to remember, however, that the root cause of a depression is not dealt with through electric shock treatment if the underlying problem is psychological or spiritual.

Psychological treatment of depression
Another means of dealing with depression

is through psychological methods, such as counseling. Individual therapy, where a counselor and a depressed person work closely together, is the most common type of counseling practiced. A counselor may strive to help a depressed person understand himself better, change negative thinking patterns, express his feelings appropriately, or reorient his life style to relieve depression.

Group counseling or talking over problems with a number of individuals is also helpful. Group therapy allows an individual to get valuable feedback and support from others experiencing similar difficulties.

Family or marriage counseling is often helpful when a person's depression stems from difficulties in the home setting. Depression may be caused or intensified by family conflict and tension. Family counselors believe everyone suffers when a family member is depressed. Therefore, it makes sense to engage the whole family in helping a loved one who is discouraged.

A distraught person named Helen sat in my office wringing her hands in despair. When I told Helen I prefer to counsel with whole families, she reacted angrily by saying, "Don't you dare drag my family into this! My family relationships are fine. This is my problem and no one can do anything about it but me." However, I learned that Helen's daughter freely talked back and her son was deep into the drug scene. Helen's husband worked extremely long hours and gave her little emotional support. When Helen was distressed, her husband told her to "snap out of it" rather than trying to understand why she was upset.

Family therapy proved to be an effective technique to bring about changes in Helen's home life. Her husband listened intently as Helen explained her need for companionship from him. New understandings emerged as channels of communication were opened up between parents and children. Her family's newly discovered insights and support were key factors in helping Helen overcome depression.

Recreation and depression

A vital therapeutic task in working with depressed individuals is to help the discouraged person become functional rather than withdrawing from his environment. Hobbies such as music, crafts, and sports provide a discouraged individual with an excellent change of pace and help a person renew his interests. Recreation enables a discouraged individual to get his mind off himself and concentrate on the external world. In addition, activities involving large muscle movements, such as jogging, tennis, and swimming, relieve muscular tension and rigidity which often accompany depression.

Recent research indicates that a regular exercise program, especially one which involves running or jogging, can have a significant therapeutic impact upon depression. Preliminary findings indicate that running and jogging cause chemical reactions which are similar to those produced by antidepressant medication.

I believe that one of the most useful antidotes for depression involves discouraged people getting their hands into the soil. Therefore, I often advise depressed patients to get busy with a hobby of gardening. Working with the soil is a marvelous way to get close to nature and to commune with the Lord. It is not necessary to have a large garden plot, since tending even a few plants can be therapeutic.

Depressed people should stay as busy as possible. Recreational activity and vocational interests allow discouraged individuals outlets for repressed emotions and avenues for creativity. This assures a depressed person that he can still function and use his talents to good advantage.

Spiritual treatment of depression

Many Christians who are depressed need counseling and guidance to clear up spiritual confusion. Guilt, self-pity, and a negative self-concept can best be handled by an understanding counselor who loves the Lord. Christian counselors bring a depth of understanding into spiritual issues which reinforce Christian convictions and enhance a person's walk with the Lord.

Christians who are depressed generally focus on the punitive side of God and completely disregard His love and concern. A lady named Laura consulted me for depression, stating a firm belief that God was punishing her. "God has already condemned me, so what's the use of trying," Laura stated. "I've done a lot of wrong things that I don't believe God could ever forgive me for." Laura was firmly entrenched into the view of a punitive God who punishes people every time they step out of line.

Depressed people like Laura commonly have a negative theology. They have memorized scores of Bible passages about God's judgment and view God as an ogre in the sky who is ready to pounce on them. They may be locked into a legalistic theology, seeing Christianity strictly as a list of dos and don'ts. Such individuals can quote dozens of verses regarding God's judgment, but are unable to produce more than a few promises relating to His love and grace. A polluted thought life accompanied by a negative theology keeps such Christians bogged down with depression.

The human mind is like a computer. Programing your computer with negative thoughts results in troublesome behavior. As garbage fed into a computer produces more rubbish, so discouraging thoughts result in depression.

People who are depressed need to get the Word of God into their minds through proper meditation.* The Word has a healing effect that can raise a person from the throes of depression. While all Scripture is profitable, a person who is discouraged should concentrate on the positive promises of God. Reading the Psalms is especially valuable during periods of discouragement.

Praise as an antidote for depression

Praising God is one of the most effective spiritual therapies for depression that has ever been discovered. Praise and depression are at opposite poles and can hardly coexist

---

The Gift of a Sound Mind, a book written by this author and published by Herald Press, contains three chapters on positive meditation techniques for Christians.

in the same vessel. Depression cannot linger very long when a Christian's mind is saturated with praises to God. Praising the Lord focuses your mind on God, encouraging an upward rather than a downward look. The Bible admonishes you to "give thanks whatever happens; for this is what God in Christ wills for you" (1 Thess. 5:18, NEB).

David recognized the value of praising the Lord when he was downhearted and circumstances seemed against him. Listen to these words of praise from the sometimes discouraged Psalmist. "Bless the Lord, O my soul: and all that is within me, bless his holy name. Bless the Lord, O my soul, and forget not all his benefits" (Ps. 103:1-2, KJV). "My praise shall be of thee in the great congregation: I will pay my vows before them that fear him" (Ps. 22:25, KJV). "Enter into his gates with thanksgiving, and into his courts with praise: be thankful unto him, and bless his name" (Ps. 100:4, KJV).

An old saying relates that you can't keep a good person down long. David illustrates this truth remarkably well as he lifted his voice in praises to God when he was depressed. Studying the Psalms reveals that David quickly replaced negative testimonies with ringing affirmations of praise and trust in the Lord. For instance, Psalm 22 begins with

David crying out, "My God, my God, why hast thou forsaken me?" The Psalmist continues by stating, "I am a worm, not a man, scorned and despised by my own people and by all mankind" (Ps. 22:6). This psalm introduces an individual locked into depression, but this same man bounces right back in Psalm 23 to affirm, "Because the Lord is my Shepherd, I have everything I need!" (Ps. 23:1).

David also expresses his discouragement in Psalm 25, "Come, Lord, and show me your mercy, for I am helpless, overwhelmed, in deep distress; my problems go from bad to worse" (Ps. 25:16-17). However, David again emerges to affirm his faith and trust in the Lord by stating, "The Lord is my light and my salvation; whom shall I fear? the Lord is the strength of my life; of whom shall I be afraid?" (Ps. 27:1, KJV).

Psalm 31 is another hymn of discouragement, as David states, "O Lord, have mercy on me in my anguish. My eyes are red from weeping; my health is broken from sorrow. I am pining away with grief; my years are shortened, drained away because of sadness. . . . I am forgotten like a dead man, like a broken and discarded pot" (Ps. 31:9-12). However, the note of victory in which David begins the next three Psalms offers a fascinating contrast, "What happiness for those whose guilt have been forgiven!" (Ps. 32:1). "Let all the joys of the godly well up in praise to the Lord, for it is right to praise him" (Ps. 33:1). "I will bless the Lord at all times: his praise shall continually be in my mouth" (Ps. 34:1, KJV).

The crowning victory over discouragement through praise comes from the lips of David in Psalm 42. "Why then be downcast? Why be discouraged and sad? Hope in God! I shall yet praise him again. Yes, I shall again praise him for his help. . . . I will meditate upon your kindness to this lovely land. . . . day by day the Lord also pours out his steadfast love upon me, and through the night I sing his songs and pray to God who gives me life" (Ps. 42:5-8).

David discovered a key to overcoming depression through praise to the Lord. This biblical solution to depression is as current as today's newspaper. Therefore, the next time you are discouraged, try praising the Lord. Praise will help lift your spirit to God, who desires to raise you from the depths of despair into the joy that is waiting for you through the avenue of praise.

Music and depression

Music is one of the most potent elements available to register an impact on people's emotions. Wholesome music that is expressed with feeling to the Lord can prevent depression or lift our spirits when we are discouraged. On the other hand, certain types of music tend to push people further into the depths of despair.

Rock-and-roll music can easily contribute to depression through the message conveyed by the lyrics. In addition, behavior such as drugs and immoral activity which often surrounds rock music can easily propel a listener into a state of depression.

Country-and-western music can also have a depressing effect on a listener. People who have a steady diet of country-and-western music may find themselves feeling discouraged as they identify with the messages conveyed by these songs. Self-pity is easily reinforced as country music projects scenes of broken relationships.

It is particularly sad when gospel music reinforces self-pity and depression. Some music describes the Christian life as a hard struggle, affirming that we will barely make it through. Gospel music which accentuates the negative does little to prevent depression or to lift the spirits of discouraged individuals.

God gives a joyful song, not a mournful dirge, to His people. "Oh, praise the Lord, for

he has listened to my pleadings! He is my
strength, my shield from every danger. I
trusted in him, and he helped me. Joy rises in
my heart until I burst out in songs of praise to
him" (Ps. 28:6-7).

"Talk with each other much about the Lord,
quoting psalms and hymns and singing sa-
cred songs, making music in your hearts to
the Lord. Always give thanks for everything
to our God and Father in the name of our
Lord Jesus Christ" (Eph. 5:19-20).

Music therapy and depression

Music therapy is currently emerging as a
new profession in the behavioral sciences.
This field introduces new dimensions for
integrating music in treatment programs
for the emotionally disturbed. Music therapists in psychiatric settings encourage music
as a hobby and inspire people to express their
troublesome emotions through music. This
profession helps discouraged people release
the songs that are hiding under the black
clouds of discouragement.

The Psalmist David was one of the first
music therapists ever to minister skillfully to
a depressed individual. David's ministry as a
music therapist to Saul is recorded in 1 Sam.
16:14-23. "But the Spirit of the Lord had left
Saul, and instead, the Lord had sent a tor-

menting spirit that filled him with depression and fear. Some of Saul's aides suggested a cure. 'We'll find a good harpist to play for you whenever the tormenting spirit is bothering you,' they said. 'The harp music will quiet you and you will soon be well again.'. . . And whenever the tormenting spirit from God troubled Saul, David would play the harp and Saul would feel better, and the evil spirit would go away."

Periods of discouragement are occasions when we generally do not feel like singing. The song of joy that readily flows from our lips in times of happiness suddenly vanishes when we are depressed. Discouragement allows Christians to identify with the people of Israel who cried out in their captivity, "Weeping, we sat by the rivers of Babylon thinking of Jerusalem. We have put away our lyres, hanging them upon the branches of the willow trees, for how can we sing?" (Ps. 137:1-3).

However, Christians also find that our God gives a song even in the dense blackness of the darkest night. His people can sing when their journey leads them into sadness and discouragement. "Yet the Lord will command his lovingkindness in the daytime, and in the night his song shall be with me" (Ps. 42:8, KJV). David said further that "he hath put a new song in my mouth, even praise unto our God" (Ps. 40:3, KJV).

Summary

The theme of this chapter is that you can do something to help yourself overcome depression. Wholesome recreation, uplifting music, and heartfelt praise to God are all positive avenues that will help lift you out of the valley of discouragement.

When personal resources fail, others stand by ready and willing to help. An understanding pastor, a supportive counselor, or a family physician all bring their special expertise to assist you in a time of discouragement.

The Bible declares that our "God is . . . a very present help in trouble" (Ps. 46:1). He rushes to the side of a depressed person, always ready to help in His own special way. The Lord revealed himself to His depressed servants in a fascinating manner that sheds further light on the treatment of depression.

The next chapter highlights some of the ways the Lord dealt with discouraged Christians in the Bible.

11

How God Intervenes
to Help Depressed People

We can learn a great deal about overcoming depression by studying the manner in which God dealt with biblical characters who were discouraged. For instance, God pioneered an important concept known as "ministering to the whole man" when He dealt with Elijah. Physical, psychological, social, and spiritual factors were all considered as God lifted Elijah from his depression. First Kings, chapter 19, reveals how this was accomplished.

"I give my beloved ones rest"
God ministered to Elijah's physical needs by encouraging him to sleep. Elijah's depression coincided with a period of physical exhaustion as he fled in fear from Queen Jezebel. His journey took him deep into the wilderness, where he literally collapsed in fatigue and exhaustion. Such a tiring excur-

sion demanded a time of rest and rejuvenation. God provided ample time for Elijah to sleep, realizing that His prophet needed considerable rest following such a fatiguing journey.

Depression and other emotional problems can readily settle upon people who are physically worn out. Some individuals tumble into depression following an illness which saps their physical strength. Others neglect their proper rest by staying up into the wee hours of the night.

A patient named Melvin sat in my office yawning, his eyelids drooping as he fought to stay awake. I asked Melvin why he was so sleepy and he replied, "I have been awake for many nights until 3:00 A.M., talking on my CB. I find this is the best time to make contact with interesting people in the area." Melvin provided an open invitation for depression to overtake him by rejecting his body's call for proper sleep.

"I don't want to talk to you; I just want to sleep," a patient who was totally worn out said to me. This person slept soundly for several days following her hospital admission. We learned she had been staying up late every night watching TV until the station signed off.

Adequate rest is essential to counteract and overcome depression. The following suggestions will help you obtain the sleep you need to ward off discouragement.

1. *Meditate on Scripture and the things of the Lord.* Someone has suggested that Christians who can't sleep should talk to the Shepherd instead of counting sheep. David said, "I lay awake at night thinking of You—of how much you have helped me—and how I rejoice through the night beneath the protecting shadow of your wings" (Ps. 63:6).

2. *Know the limits of your body and mind.* Every person needs a certain amount of sleep to function properly. Discover your level of sleep for optimal functioning, and don't push yourself beyond these limits.

3. *Try to relax before you go to sleep.* Make a mental search of your body to determine if any part of you is uptight or tense. Encouraging your body to relax can be a helpful prelude to sleep.

4. *Make a practice not to stay up into the late-night hours.* God provides the night for sleep to renew your mind and body. "It is vain for you to rise up early, to sit up late, to eat the bread of sorrows: for so he giveth his beloved sleep" (Ps. 127:2, KJV).

A motto on the wall of my grandparents' bedroom stated, "Early to bed, early to rise, makes a man healthy, wealthy, and wise." My grandparents, who followed this practice, enjoyed excellent health and lived to a ripe old age.

5. *Consult your doctor to discover if there are physical reasons why you are not sleeping.* Medication may be of assistance if sleeplessness persists. Christians may react to inducing sleep through chemicals, but it is probably more dangerous to go for long periods without obtaining adequate rest.

Some psychiatric hospitals have instituted programs of sleep therapy for depressed patients who are worn out. Medication induces sound sleep which may last for several days. (Doesn't that sound good?) Many patients show immediate improvement from their depression upon awakening from a deep sleep.

"Rise Up and Eat"

An angel came by Elijah's side as he slept and told him, "Get up and eat! He looked around and saw some bread baking on hot stones, and a jar of water! So he ate and drank and lay down again" (1 Kings 19:5-6).

It is probable that Elijah merely nibbled at the food presented to him because he temporarily lost his appetite while he was depressed. Consequently, the angel persisted by inviting Elijah to eat again. The food that Elijah consumed was essential to give him adequate energy for a long journey back to civilization.

Some Christians are convinced that depressed periods are excellent occasions for fasting. However, this is generally a poor time to deny food to the body. A depressed person should eat properly to sustain his physical and emotional health. The Lord recognized this truth as He encouraged Elijah to maintain a proper diet during his time of discouragement.

"I can assure you that you are not alone"

God ministered to Elijah's emotional and social needs through encouragement and support. The Lord was a good listener, as He allowed Elijah to ventilate his worries and concerns. God helped Elijah with his feelings of isolation by promising him that he was not alone, because there were "7,000 men in Israel who have never bowed to Baal or kissed him" (1 Kings 19:18).

"I will surround you with my presence"

God also dealt with Elijah's spiritual welfare in a special way. The Lord instructed Elijah to seclude himself on a mountain peak where His presence would pass by. Wind, fire, and an earthquake shook the mountain in rapid sequence as Elijah quietly lingered before the Lord. However, it was a gentle whisper that assured Elijah that God was still with him and he had a valuable ministry to perform for the Lord.

God's Meaningful Message to Job

God also ministered to Job in a particularly effective manner during his discouragement. God directly intervened with skilled insight and competent understandings designed to raise Job from depression. Here is advice directly from the heart of God to a discouraged individual.

"Be mature"

The first statement that the Lord made to Job was "Stand up like a man and brace yourself for the battle" (Job 40:7). The Lord recognized that Job was acting immaturely by wallowing in self-pity and blaming God for his problems. God encouraged Job to put away childish actions and behave like a man.

The strong medicine God handed to Job is hard to swallow. However, God may admonish us in a similar manner when we are depressed by saying, *"Grow up! Stop acting in such an immature manner! Don't you realize it's childish to wrap yourself up in self-pity and discouragement?"* Paul also encourages Christians along this line when he says,

"When I was a child, I spake as a child, I understood as a child, I thought as a child: but when I became a man, I put away childish things" (1 Cor. 13:11, KJV).

"Stop blaming me for your problems"

God asked Job, "Are you going to discredit my justice and condemn me, so that you can say that you are right?" (Job 40:8). In other words, God was saying, "Why are you criticizing me and blaming me for your predicament? Who are you to question my judgment by saying that you are right and I am wrong?"

Many depressed people who criticize God and blame Him for their problems need to pay attention to God's admonition to Job. Your recovery from depression will be much quicker if you stop blaming God for your predicament and take an honest look at what you can do to change.

"Stop to recognize my greatness"

God emphasized Job's limitations in relationship to His greatness by asking Job some very pointed and provocative questions. God said to Job, "Where were you when I laid the foundations of the earth? . . . Have you ever once commanded the morning to appear? . . . Can you hold back the stars? . . . Have you explored the springs from which the seas

come? . . . Where does light come from . . .
Or tell me about darkness. . . . Can you
shout to the clouds and make it rain? Can you
make lightning appear and cause it to strike
as you direct it?" (Job 38).

God emphasized His greatness and majesty
to point out the ridiculous nature of Job's self-
pity. We also bow our heads in shame when
we realize we have become totally wrapped
up in our own little world of problems. Breaking out of ourselves to realize God's greatness
is a step forward in overcoming discouragement.

"Notice my care for all creation"

The Lord draws several illustrations from
the animal kingdom to impress certain truths
upon Job's mind. These lessons from nature
speak directly to Job because of the flocks
and herds he owned. God's concern for His
creation is symbolized in this way: "Who
makes the wild donkeys wild? I have placed
them in the wilderness and given them salt
plains to live in. For they hate the noises
of the city and want no drivers shouting at
them! The mountain ranges are their pas-
tureland; there they search for every blade of
grass" (Job 39:5-8).

God emphasizes His consideration for the
beasts of the field to demonstrate His love for

Job. A depressed person needs to comprehend the concern God has for him. Jesus assured us of God's watchful attention when He said, "Look at the birds! . . . they don't need to sow or reap or store up food—for your heavenly Father feeds them. And you are far more valuable to him than they are" (Matt. 6:26). When you are depressed, you need to realize you are more valuable than the delicate lilies of the field. You are worth far more than the life of a petite sparrow that God cares for so tenderly.

"You don't have all the answers"

God helped Job realize it was not necessary to have answers for all of life's perplexing questions. God said, "Do you—God's critic—have the answers?" (Job 40:2). Job replied simply, "I am nothing—how could I ever find the answers? I lay my hand upon my mouth in silence. I have said too much already" (Job 40:4-5).

We sometimes second-guess God as Job did by conjuring up all kinds of difficult questions. We may wonder why God allows so much suffering in the world. Why are some children born crippled? Why does famine, hunger, and disease grip so much of the world's populace? For what purposes are children mentally retarded?

A little handicapped boy came struggling

down the aisle to greet me following a message I had delivered. One of the most touching moments of my life occurred as he looked up at me and said, "Good morning, mister. How are you today?" This little fellow's cheery salutation was the most inspiring event that happened to me that day. He ministered to me with that simple but powerful greeting. People who wonder why he is handicapped cannot offer a satisfactory rationale. However, his sweet spirit is more noticeable than his weak limbs. I am certain this young fellow encourages his family regularly in the way he ministered to me. Only the Lord knows how many people will be strengthened by this lad, who radiates God's love in the midst of adversity.

Magdalene Crocker's meaningful song "I Don't Need to Understand" shows us how to deal with the fact that we will never have answers to all of life's difficult questions:

I don't need to understand, I just need to hold His hand.
I don't need to ever ask the reason why.
For I know He'll make a way thru the night and thru the day;
I don't need to understand, I just need to hold His hand.[1]

---

[1]"I Don't Need to Understand," by Magdalene Crocker. Copyright © 1964 by Faith Music Co. All rights reserved. Used by permission.

"There are some things in my life I just don't understand," a young lady named Sandy stated sadly. Sandy was barely able to function, as she was mired down in deep introspection. This discouraged young woman became bogged down with depression by trying to find answers to all of life's perplexing questions. She looked inside herself for reasons behind everything that had occurred in her life. She questioned God's purpose for her trials, believing He had forsaken her. Recognizing God was in control of her destiny and that He would reveal answers to her in His timing proved to be a real struggle for Sandy.

I do not mean to imply that we should not seek to understand ourselves or find answers to life's pressing questions. Occasional inner reflection and introspection is healthy, and it enhances our inner person. However, there are some questions that should be left in the hands of the Lord. There are times when we need to stop wrestling with the perplexing problems that plague our minds, as we get on with the business of living.

Developing a sensitivity to God's greatness and love allows us to share Job's confession to the Lord. "I know that you can do anything and that no one can stop you. You asked who it was who had so foolishly denied your providence. It is I. I was talking about things I knew nothing about and did not understand, things far too wonderful for me" (Job 42:2-3).

At the time of this confession, Job was ready to put aside depression and resume a productive life. We can identify with him as he recognizes that he went too far in trying to understand all of life's mysteries, for "I have said too much already" (Job 40:5).

Summary

God wants to deal with you in His unique style just as He touched the lives of His servants of old. God's ministry to depressed biblical characters may be just what you require to escape the stronghold of discouragement. Here is a summary of God's prescriptions and admonitions to depressed individuals:

1. Maintain your physical strength through adequate rest and nourishment.
2. Remember that you are not alone.
3. Recall that His presence surrounds you at all times.
4. Put away immature actions and become a mature adult.
5. Don't blame God for your problems.
6. Stop and recognize the Lord's greatness.
7. Take note of His care for all creation.
8. Remember that you don't have all the answers.

God brought His help to Job with a ministry designed to cut to the heart of his discouragement. At the same time, three well-intentioned comforters sat with Job, doing their best to help him through this crisis. Let us turn now to the intervention of Job's friends, as we examine some of their successful and unsuccessful ways to help people who are depressed.

12

Lessons from Job's Comforters

It is easy to come down hard on Job's comforters by finding fault with their approach to a depressed individual. However, people who are critical of Job's comforters tend to overlook the positive characteristics they possessed. For instance, they came to Job at a time of critical need, traveling a distance to be with him. They sat for seven days and nights without speaking a word, quietly sharing Job's misery. (Have you ever heard of a better example of nonverbal communication?) While their statements to Job were not always accurate or helpful, their motives were good, and their comments were designed to alleviate Job's depression.

In spite of these factors, Job called his friends "miserable comforters," pointing out their blunders in trying to lift him from his wretched condition. Let us look at how Job's friends dealt with him, analyzing why they were unsuccessful in helping Job escape from discouragement. We will use the illustration of Job's friends to highlight some of the "do nots" of ministering to depressed people.

1. *Job's friends accused him of being a sinner, stating that his depression was a result of sinful behavior.*

It is common for Christians to be persuaded that depression always stems from sin. You may have heard fellow believers say, "If you are depressed, it is because you have sinned. You need to confess your sin to God before you will get over your depression." While sin may cause discouragement, we cannot always assume that depression is due to sin. We have already noted that physical, psychological, and social factors must be considered along with spiritual causes of depression.

Telling a Christian that sin is making him depressed may intensify his feelings of guilt, making it harder for the individual to recover. Implying that he is a sinner because he is depressed may push a discouraged Christian deeper into the throes of despair.

It is easy to assume that a depressed person's problem is sin and that he will recover when wrongdoing is uncovered and confessed. Job's comforters approached him from every possible angle to hammer this message into their friend. Here are some examples of their statements regarding this issue: "Go to God and confess your sins to him" (5:8). "Get rid of your sins and leave all iniquity behind you" (11:14). "Your sins are telling your mouth what to say" (15:5). These are only a few of a number of occasions where Job's friends emphatically declared that his problems resulted from sin. In fact, by Job's count, his friends pronounced him a guilty sinner on ten distinct occasions (19:3).

Telling Job he was a sinner didn't relieve his depression. Job was convinced of his innocence and confidently proclaimed that sin was not his problem. Job declared, "Tell me, what have I done wrong? . . . Stop assuming my guilt, for I am righteous" (6:24, 29). Again Job stated, "This is my case: I know that I am righteous" (13:18). Over and over Job affirmed that sin was not his problem, and he came down hard on his comforters for assuming that sinful behavior was at the heart of his depression.

2. *Job's comforters assumed that God was punishing him for his wrongdoing.*

The belief that God was dishing out harsh discipline because of Job's sin came through clearly in the advice Job's comforters offered. "How enviable the man whom God corrects! Oh, do not despise the chastening of the Lord when you sin" (5:17). Again, his comforters declared, "Listen! God is doubtless punishing you far less than you deserve!" (11:6). His comforters declared further, "Stop and think! Have you ever known a truly good and innocent person who was punished? Experience teaches that it is those who sow sin and trouble who harvest the same" (4:7-9).

A study of the Scripture reveals it was erroneous to believe God was punishing Job for wrongdoing. God allowed Job's trials, but it was Satan who bombarded him with problems. God did not see a sinner to be punished when He looked at Job. God praised Job as He asked Satan, "Have you noticed my servant Job? He is the finest man in all earth—a good man who fears God and will have nothing to do with evil" (1:8). The positive testimony of Scripture regarding Job reveals that Job did not sin or revile God in spite of all his losses (1:22).

Many Christians believe God punishes people by making them sick. A Christian lady prayed, "Thank you, Lord, for making me sick." A gentleman testified, "The Lord is bringing depression upon me to see how much I can bear." Another individual stated, "God is punishing me for something I did wrong by bringing this terrible depression on me."

Believing that God is a punitive Father

who punishes people by making them sick is a view that is very difficult for me to comprehend. God doesn't knock His children down every time they do something wrong. This view ignores God's tender, loving nature and fills people with anxiety that God might strike them down at any moment.

Did God punish or condemn biblical characters who experienced extreme discouragement? Never! God's ministry to Elijah provided for his needs without condemnation. Job was rescued from depression and his fortune restored. David received forgiveness from God's hand, and Peter was lifted from discouragement. God's ministry to a depressed person is one of forgiveness, love, and restoration. When you are discouraged, you need to realize that God wants to pick you up rather than strike you down.

3. *Job's friends closely scrutinized his behavior, frantically searching for specific causes they could pin his depression on.*

Job's comforters were quick to lecture him on all the things he needed to change. For instance, they implied that Job was depressed because he had accumulated too much money. "This wicked man is fat and rich, and has lived in conquered cities after killing off its citizens. But he will not continue to be rich, or to extend his possessions. . . . Let him no longer trust in foolish riches; let him no longer deceive himself, for the money he trusts will be his only reward" (15:27-29, 31). "If you give up your lust for money, and throw your gold away, then the Almighty himself shall be your treasure; he will be your precious silver!" (22:24-25).

Job's friends also told him he was sick because he was selfish and declined to do good works. They said, "You must have refused to loan money to needy friends unless they gave you all their clothing as a pledge— yes, you must have stripped them to the bone. You must have refused water to the thirsty, and bread to the starving" (22:6-7).

Job's comforters accused him of favoring the rich and shunning poor people. "But no doubt you gave men of importance anything they wanted, and let the wealthy live wherever they chose. You sent widows away without helping them, and broke the arms of orphans. That is why you are now surrounded by traps and sudden fears, and darkness and waves of horror" (22:8-10).

Job again disagreed with his friends' analyses of his problem. Job said, "For I, as an honest judge, helped the poor in their need, and the fatherless who had no one to help them. . . . I caused the widows' hearts to

sing for joy. . . . I served as eyes for the blind
and feet for the lame. I was as a father to the
poor, and saw to it that even strangers
received a fair trial" (29:12-16). Job offered
further rebuttal to his comforters with these
words, "If I have hurt the poor or caused
widows to weep, or refused food to hungry
orphans—. . . or if I have seen anyone freez-
ing and not given them clothing . . . or if I
have taken advantage of an orphan. . . . Let
my shoulder be wrenched out of place!"
(31:16-23).

It is tempting to scrutinize closely a depressed person's behavior under our judgmental and critical microscopes. It is easy to
analyze every word and action with a fine-
toothed comb. We naturally want to change
those things that are wrong about a depressed
person so they can be happy again. It is easy
to reply quickly as Job's friends did, "I have
examined your behavior, and I have the
answer to your problems" (20:2, author's
paraphrase).

I occasionally catch myself pressuring depressed people to hurry up and change. I
once counseled with a depressed girl named
Barbara, who seemed to have many personal
characteristics that needed to be altered. I
became rather picky as I pointed out problems for Barbara to work on. My advice was

good, but she wasn't ready to receive my insights. She resisted my efforts to transform her as I pushed harder and harder. I panicked as Barbara became more depressed under the pressure I was applying. I fortunately was able to change my tactics by focusing on Barbara's strengths rather than her problems. This proved to be a much better way to help this young lady overcome depression.

4. *Job's friends provided practically no support or encouragement to their distressed brother.*

As we have seen, Job's friends majored in minors. Their statements resounded with negativism rather than communicating support and understanding. Their ability to share deeply with Job in his distress was wanting, as these men stood aloof, piously judging his behavior. Little effort was made to sustain Job or build up his shaky self-esteem. Even Job's wife told him to curse God and die (2:9).

Job's feedback to his comforters indicates the lack of support he felt from them. Job stated, "One should be kind to a fainting friend, but you have accused me without the slightest fear of God. My brother, you have proved as unreliable as a brook" (6:14-15).

"You are doctors who don't know what you are doing" (13:4). "All of you please go away; for I do not find a wise man among you" (17:10).

Job called his friends "miserable comforters" and added this note of satire and irony: "What wonderful helpers you are! And how you have encouraged me in my great need! How you have enlightened my stupidity! What wise things you have said! How did you ever think of all these brilliant comments?" (26:2-4). In summing up the efforts of his comforters to help him in his misery, Job said, "Oh, that there was someone to listen to me and try to see my side of this argument" (31:35). Job felt misunderstood, alone, and frustrated as a result of the efforts of his friends to comfort him. He pointed out that their advice was of little value to him, since they were not supportive.

The Lord was also displeased with Job's friends, telling them they were wrong to condemn Job by calling him a sinner. Listen to God's message to Job's comforters: "You have not been right in what you have said about me, as my servant Job was. Now take seven young bulls and seven rams and go to my servant Job and offer a burnt offering for yourselves; and my servant Job will pray for you, and I will accept his prayer on your behalf, and won't destroy you as I should because of your sin, your failure to speak rightly concerning my servant Job" (42:7-8).

Summary

It is easy to drift into behavior patterns employed by Job's comforters when dealing with depressed friends and loved ones. However, these techniques seldom bear fruit in lifting a troubled individual out of his crisis. Some of the "do nots" to remember when dealing with depressed people are summarized below in light of the approach of Job's comforters.

1. *Do not imply that a fellow believer is depressed because of wrongdoing.*

We have seen that depression may stem from sinful behavior. In addition, there are times when it is appropriate to confront sin in a fellow believer's life. However, a head-to-head confrontation with sin in another individual requires a keen sensitivity to the Spirit's leading and the needs of a fellow believer. Overall, one must remember it is the Holy Spirit, not another individual, who convicts of sin.

A general rule to follow is to avoid a dogmatic approach which singles out sin as the exclusive cause of someone's depression. A lecture which includes judgmental statements such as "You are depressed because of sinful behavior" may drive a person deeper into discouragement.

2. *Do not imply that God is punishing a fellow believer.*

Such an implication generally reinforces a warped view of God as an ogre in the sky, ready to pounce on people who step out of line. Intensifying guilt by implying that depression is God's judgment for wrongdoing drives a person deeper into discouragement.

3. *Do not lecture or point out all the areas a depressed individual needs to change.*

Depressed people generally berate themselves as they bring imperfections and shortcomings into sharp focus. Pointing out problems and deficiencies may make a discouraged individual kick himself all the harder as he thinks about his errors.

4. *Do not overlook a depressed person's need for support.*

Your depressed friend or loved one has many needs. You are in a key position to minister to that individual as you are led by the Holy Spirit. Read the next chapter to discover how you can reach out in positive ways to depressed individuals.

13

How to Free People from the Vise Grip of Depression

We have discussed several unsuccessful ways Job's friends tried to help him overcome his depression. With these "do nots" in mind, let us look at constructive ways of dealing with people who are downhearted.

Ten Positive Approaches to Helping Depressed People

1. *Offer support, understanding, and encouragement.*

Merrill Womach, a Christian man who was seriously burned in an airplane crash, tells of the depression he went through during the difficult days of his recovery. Some Christian friends stopped in to visit at a particularly dark moment when everything seemed hopeless. There was something about the fellowship of these Christians that helped Womack snap out of his depression. As he analyzed what helped him, Womack concluded it was his friends' interest, support, and understanding that tipped the scales. They did not give him advice or offer a lecture. Their presence said, "We care." The concern, warmth, and loving attitude conveyed by these nurturing Christians encouraged their downcast brother. They accomplished more than medication or therapy could have done at that particular point in time, simply by being supportive.

A Christian is to minister in tenderness and love to discouraged people. The Bible says, "With this news bring cheer to all discouraged ones. Encourage those who are afraid. Tell them, 'Be strong, fear not, for your God is coming to destroy your enemies'" (Isa. 35:3-4). The Word tells us further to "comfort those who are frightened; take tender care of those who are weak; and be patient with everyone" (1 Thess. 5:14).

2. *Be a good listener.*

It is helpful simply to allow a depressed person to ventilate and talk about his problems. Successful counselors are good listeners, and many people benefit by being able to talk out their concerns with someone who will listen. Many people who come for counseling say, "Thank you for listening to my problems.

I feel better after being able to talk things out."

You don't have to be a trained counselor to grant a discouraged person a listening ear. Being someone who is concerned enough to sit down and listen may allow you to provide just the right therapy for a discouraged individual.

3. *Be concerned, but do not offer sympathy.*

To extend love, understanding, and support is helpful to someone who is depressed. However, offering sympathy may drive a discouraged individual deeper into self-pity. Don't say, "Oh, you poor thing, you have it so hard. I've never heard such a sad story in my life."

It is tempting to fall into a trap of offering sympathy to a depressed person. Distressing life situations often provoke a responsive chord of sympathy within a listener. However, while we should be concerned and let a depressed person know we care, to offer sympathy is likely to reinforce discouragement.

4. *Help a depressed person regain his interests and resume his responsibilities.*

Depressed people who come into our hospital often head for the nearest couch or chair. They would sit or lay for hours if we allowed them to. However, our staff realizes that depressed people need to be gently and firmly urged and nudged toward activity. Therefore, we immediately begin a program of activities designed to bring a withdrawn person back into the mainstream of life.

Doing everything for a discouraged individual can be a crucial mistake. A depressed lady I counsel with calls loudly for her mother's help every time she feels discouraged. Mother dutifully comes to her daughter's rescue by cleaning the house and caring for her children. This depressed lady relaxes while mother knocks herself out by working. Reinforcing dependency and helplessness in this manner is unhealthy for a depressed person.

Discouraged people need to resume their responsibilities and interests as quickly as possible. A depressed housewife may require encouragement from her family to assume housekeeping chores. A depressed husband may need a great deal of reassurance to get back to work. A Christian can help a depressed friend get into the swing of life by inviting him out to dinner or church. Finding ways to participate in mutually enjoyable activities with a depressed individual may motivate him to get moving again.

We have seen that God helped a discouraged individual resume his activities when He dealt with Elijah. God ministered to Elijah's physical, emotional, and spiritual needs, then gave him a task, telling Elijah to "go back by the desert road to Damascus; and when you arrive, anoint Hazael to be king of Syria. Then anoint . . . Elisha . . . to replace you as my prophet" (1 Kings 19:15-16). This assignment was a key intervention that motivated Elijah to resume his interests and reactivate his ministry for the Lord.

5. *Help a depressed person think of others beside himself.*

Depressed people who are self-centered need assistance to get their mind off themselves and onto others. A depressed person can be helped by thinking about meeting other people's needs. For instance, requesting a depressed individual to help you in some way affirms them as a worthwhile person with abilities to contribute to other people's lives.

6. *Minister to a depressed person's spiritual needs.*

Depression is a time when God seems far away and one's spiritual life is in the doldrums. There is little interest in spiritual activities or faith that God will answer prayer.

195

Other Christians can help a depressed person reach God by praying with and for him. Don't be disturbed if a discouraged individual does not immediately respond to your efforts to help him. He may not be ready to pray or reach out to God at that particular moment. Don't cram spiritual things down his throat.

Reading the Bible with a depressed person gets the Scripture into his mind, where the Word can minister to inner needs. This may provide a spark of faith that will assist a discouraged individual to reach out to the Lord, tapping into the spiritual resources available in God.

7. *Be firm, but not angry or sarcastic, in your approach to a depressed person.*

Firmness is often required in dealing with depressed individuals. Depressed people may do practically nothing if left to their own devices. Therefore, they need a great deal of support and encouragement, and sometimes a push, to get moving again.

Your approach to a depressed person may be a vital ingredient in his recovery. Always be certain you are responding to a discouraged person's needs rather than to your requirements. For instance, don't approach a downhearted individual with an attitude that says, "I'm sick and tired of you being this way, so I am making an appointment for you to see a doctor." It's just as bad for you to say, "You make me sick, laying around the house all day! Cut out this foolishness and do something constructive." You will obtain better results with an attitude that says, "I know it's hard for you to do what is right, so I will help you take positive steps to overcome your problems."

8. *Encourage a depressed person to look beyond his feelings.*

This principle is difficult to accomplish, because depressed individuals are locked into their emotions. Listening to a depressed person lets you know how much they respond to their moods. Depressed people say things like, "My feelings tell me not to get up in the morning; I don't feel like going to work; it doesn't seem like I'm a Christian any more. I just don't feel good."

We can deal more effectively with depression when we understand the fickle nature of our feelings. Emotions simply cannot be trusted as a guiding force for a person's life. Being governed by our feelings will lead us down a path of instability and insecurity.

What events would transpire in your life if you constantly gave into your feelings?

Imagine what would happen if you said, "I don't feel like going to work today, so I'll just stay home. I don't feel like attending church, so I'll go fishing instead. I don't feel like getting out of bed, so I'll just sleep in."

Depressed people need guidance to live in the realm of fact rather than feeling. It is helpful to recognize that Christianity is not based on fickle feelings, but rather on God's unshakable Word. God's Word is based on fact, not feeling. The Lord says we are saved through faith. Therefore, an individual who has invited Christ into his life is redeemed, even though he doesn't always feel like he is a Christian.

God's Word is a solid foundation you can build your life on. God's statements are a "lamp to guide my feet and a light on my path" (Ps. 119:105, NEB). However, feelings are like the shifting, drifting sands that are here today and gone tomorrow.

Depressed people need help to do what is right even though they don't feel like behaving properly. Waiting to be motivated by fickle feelings will result in an unproductive life. A good principle to underscore at this point is that good feelings follow correct behavior. Launch out in faith on the promises of God and your feelings will catch up to your positive actions.

9. *Assist a depressed person to obtain professional counseling when indicated.*

A person who does not respond to the loving support and encouragement of family and friends may need professional counseling. Of course, it is difficult to establish an arbitrary time period to wait before encouraging a person to seek counseling. However, an individual who continues to be depressed for a month or longer probably needs professional assistance.

Where can a depressed person go for guidance? A medical doctor can offer valuable aid. A physician can check for medical problems that may cause depression, prescribe medication if indicated and offer supportive counseling.

A pastor is also a good resource for an individual experiencing depression. Pastors offer spiritual guidance and encouragement that can be of inestimable value to a depressed person. A pastor with expertise in counseling can also help a depressed person untangle the web of emotional problems immobilizing him.

Engaging a Christian counselor is like enlisting an ally to help in times of discouragement. Professionals trained in the disciplines of psychiatry, psychology, social work, or pastoral counseling bring a vast source of knowledge and expertise to bear on emotional problems such as depression. A Christian should be vitally concerned about locating a counselor who knows the Lord. Unfortunately, Christian counselors are limited in number, and there are vast areas of the country not being served by counselors who are believers. However, it is worth traveling to locate a counselor who loves the Lord and can assist with spiritual dilemmas along with emotional and psychological disorders.

A short inpatient stay may be required when depression has sent its roots deep into the soil of an individual's life. Inpatient care affords an opportunity for intensive therapy along with a structured program to help depressed people get moving. Once again, a Christian hospital offering psychiatric services is to be preferred over those which lack Christian values.

10. *A deeply discouraged individual needs a message of hope.*

There is hope for depressed people, even when discouragement seems to have a tenacious grip upon its victim. Discouraged individuals can be helped to change negative thinking patterns and escape depression. Deeply discouraged individuals frequently respond positively when they are assured that depression is a universal phenomena.

A depressed individual needs to realize clearly that he is not the only person who gets discouraged. In counseling, I strongly project the view that depression has a positive prognosis and it can be overcome. My clients often react to such a message with a startled look and respond, "You mean other people get depressed and I can get over this?" Helping a person realize he can recover from discouragement frees him to take steps in a positive direction.

Christians have a source of hope to offer depressed people. Jesus represents an optimistic outlook when everything looks dark and dismal. What a precious privilege to be able to administer hope through Jesus Christ to people traveling through the valley of despair.

Summary

You may hold the key to someone's escape from depression. It is possible that God wishes to use you as a channel of His love and blessing as you comfort, support, and pray for a depressed person. Keep the following guidelines firmly in mind as you reach out to discouraged individuals.

1. Offer support, understanding and encouragement.
2. Be a good listener.
3. Be concerned, but not overly sympathetic.
4. Help a depressed person regain his interests and resume his responsibilities.
5. Encourage a depressed individual to think about other people.
6. Minister to a discouraged person's spiritual needs.
7. Be firm, but not angry or sarcastic.
8. Encourage a depressed person to look beyond his feelings.
9. Don't hesitate to refer the depressed individual to a professional counselor.
10. Offer a message of hope.

14

Dealing with Situations That Seem Hopeless

Sometimes depression shoots roots deep within, keeping its victim in a stranglehold. Positive messages of affirmation and assurance simply bounce off the impenetrable barriers created by depression. People may become so overwhelmed by hopelessness and despair that suicide seems to be the only way of escape from their dilemma.

Statistics reveal that at least 35,000 Americans commit suicide every year. However, this data merely represents a tip of the iceberg, for many suicidal deaths are labeled as "accidental" or "resulting from natural causes." Surprisingly, suicide has leapfrogged up the list to take its place as a prominent cause of death among teen-agers and young adults. Furthermore, Christians are frequently counted among the ranks of suicidal victims, as scores of discouraged believers decide that life is no longer worth living.

Tips for Assessing Suicidal Risk

The following suggestions are presented to guide your actions should you encounter a friend or loved one who is contemplating suicide.

1. *Don't be reluctant to inquire about suicidal intentions.*

A key question, "Have you ever contemplated suicide?" should be addressed to all deeply discouraged individuals. Unfortunately, people are generally reluctant to direct such a provocative question to a distressed individual. It is erroneous to believe that mentioning suicide implants self-destructive ideas in the mind of a depressed individual.

However, addressing this issue is generally more positive and supportive than sidestepping the matter because of fear. An individual who is contemplating suicide needs to talk about his dilemma with a supportive listener. Your inquiry regarding the possibility of self-destructive thoughts may open the door for this to occur. You give a powerful message that says, "I care deeply about your welfare," when you inquire about suicidal potential in a deeply discouraged believer.

2. *Don't be fooled by the popular assumption that "people who talk about suicide never kill themselves."*

This false notion regarding suicide has been lurking around for a long time. Unfortunately, too many individuals have naively accepted this myth at face value. In actuality, people who openly talk about suicidal intentions are frequently high-risk candidates for self-destructive behavior. Individuals who threaten self-harm are generally begging for help, and should receive the services they require promptly.

3. *Ascertain if the afflicted individual has developed a suicide plan.*

Some people have vague and uncertain ideas about how they might harm themselves. They may declare, "I have thought about hurting myself, but I'm not sure how to go about it." Others may relate, "I feel like doing something to myself, but I'm really too much of a chicken to take any action along this line."

Obviously, individuals in these categories are less of a risk than someone with a loaded gun or a cache of pills at their fingertips. Therefore, the risk increases significantly when someone presents a highly developed action plan. However, don't take unnecessary chances, for anyone who contemplates suicide should receive immediate assistance.

4. *Assess the degree of hopelessness involved.*

Statements indicating overwhelming gloom and despair may spill from the lips of a suicidal individual. "Life is over, there's nothing left for me to live for," such individuals may state. "I manage to contaminate everyone I come in touch with. My family and everyone else would be much better off without me. I don't deserve to live, because I have made so many stupid mistakes."

Sometimes people take elaborate measures to put their houses in order just prior to a self-destructive effort. Be alert for someone who gives away prized possessions, buys additional life insurance, or makes profuse apologies for past transgressions. Such activities may earmark a distressed individual who has numbered his days.

Where to Go for Help

Like a newborn baby's arrival, psychiatric emergencies rarely occur during the normal office hours of most community agencies. Therefore, twenty-four-hour crisis intervention programs have sprung up throughout the country. Check under "Mental Health" or "Crisis Intervention" to determine if your area has these services available.

Fortunately, some communities recognize the value of a loving and empathic Christian approach to individuals in crisis. For instance, "Contact Ministries" are generally sponsored by churches and staffed by individuals who have received basic training in counseling techniques. "Contact" volunteers stand ready to lend a listening ear or make a referral to a specialized community resource.

Hopelessness Strikes Biblical Personalities

Jesus' infamous disciple, Judas Iscariot, represented a biblical character who sank deep into the pit of hopelessness and despair. Undoubtedly, Judas didn't anticipate that his ill-conceived betrayal plan would actually culminate in Jesus' crucifixion. "Surely He will perform another miracle and escape from His enemies," Judas probably rationalized.

However, such an optimistic forecast was not about to occur. Judas was horrified as he faced the stark reality that Jesus was dead. Furthermore, his actions furnished a key link in the chain of events surrounding Christ's execution.

A thick-black cloud of hopelessness and despair moved in to engulf Judas. Jesus' battered disciple grasped his betrayal award, rushed to the high priest's office, and slammed the money to the floor. Returning the betrayal reward was his last-ditch effort to soothe a conscience which nagged and harassed Judas since Jesus' death. Perhaps the priest would absolve him of responsibility, he may have thought, and he could gain some peace of mind.

However, the Jewish religious leaders refused to cooperate with Judas's frantic efforts to undo the mess he had created. "But I have betrayed an innocent man," Judas screamed at his conspirators. "That's your problem" was the chilly response from the hard-hearted Jewish leaders (Matt. 27:4).

This frigid reception dashed Judas's final hopes, pushing him to the brink of despair. The overloaded circuits of his troubled mind simply could not endure any more pressure. The hopelessness and desperation staring back at Judas represented just the right stimulus for him to conjure up a plan of self-destruction.

Unfortunately, Judas decided to take matters into his own hands rather than seeking help regarding his problem. How could Judas have so quickly forgotten Jesus' loving and compassionate approach to imperfect humanity? Hadn't he been present when Jesus pardoned the woman taken in adultery? How could he have ignored Jesus' teaching on forgiveness? Hadn't he heard Jesus declare that "he who is sick needs a physician"? Now Judas had become the ill person who needed a doctor.

We want to shout, "Stop!" to this distressed man. We would rush to assure Judas that Jesus loves him, and that he can be forgiven. If only someone could have persuaded this fallen disciple to discuss his dilemma with a supportive listener.

Unfortunately, no one was available to intervene in Judas's behalf. There were no loving Christians present to assure Judas that somehow it would all work out satisfactorily. The only message Judas heard was his battered brain telling him to do away with himself.

The watchman at Philippi's jail is another biblical personality who faced a severe life crisis. However, this story has a favorable conclusion, as the jail keeper reached out to accept a loving crisis ministry.

The occupants of Philippi's prison were startled by a massive earthquake that occurred while Paul and Silas took part in a concert to the Lord. Once-secure shackles broke loose, and foreboding iron bars snapped like toothpicks under the earthquake's jarring force. Fear and trembling gripped the jailer, who impulsively concluded that his charges had all escaped. This fearful man spontaneously decided to take matters into his own hands, assuming he would be executed for allowing a mass exit. The jailer pulled his sword and pointed it toward his heart as Paul's reassuring voice pierced the blackness of night. "Don't do it! We are all here!" Paul emphatically declared (Acts 16:28).

This forceful statement calmed the jailkeeper's jangled nerves, clearly letting him know that things were not as bad as they seemed. "Look around you—the prisoners have not escaped. Your life is not in jeopardy as you fear" was the essence of Paul's reassuring message. The apostle moved with boldness and confidence to allay swiftly the jailer's worst anxieties and apprehensions.

Paul's hopeful message to the distraught jailer should be heard by every person who is contemplating suicide. This reassuring statement still rings true: "Stop! Don't do that. The problems that seem so overwhelming can be solved. Your situation is not as hopeless as you believe."

The jailkeeper responded openly to Paul's optimistic message. He threw down his sword and ran through the jail, reassuring himself that the prisoners had not escaped. Imagine his joy and gratitude when he recognized that all was not lost. Paul and Silas, men who were earlier whipped and scourged in malice, responded with an act of love and mercy that literally saved the jailer's life.

Paul and Silas might have readily opted to proceed without further interaction with the jailer. They had saved a man's life. The suicidal crisis was over—an individual had been plucked from the brink of despair. Shackles that had once been strong and secure now lay helpless at the apostles' feet. Nothing prevented them from turning their backs on the stark jail scene to pursue careers that had been rudely interrupted. One could hardly blame them for wishing the jailer a fond "good night" and making their way back to a more civilized existence.

Counselors who interact with self-destructive individuals frequently stop after performing a crisis ministry. The goal of crisis intervention from a secular perspective is to restore an individual to his previous level of functioning. Mental health workers breathe a sigh of relief when depression lifts and the suicide crisis is over. Their error is one of omission—they stop short of offering the individual a solid anchor that holds fast and provides much-needed stability when future tempests strike.

The wise apostles, however, freely offered more than an emergency service, as they ministered to the jailer's emotional and spiritual needs. After all, it was highly unlikely that Paul and Silas would have been available to perform a similar rescue operation the next time around. Who could have guaranteed that the jailer would not reach for a sword or a pill bottle when a future crisis threatened?

Paul and Silas skillfully pointed the jailer to the one who promises to accompany His people through every emergency. "Sirs, what must I do to be saved?" inquired the jailer. "Believe on the Lord Jesus Christ and you will be saved," came the swift response (Acts 16:30-31).

Paul's optimistic message also projected hope for the jailer's family. "You shall be saved . . . and your household." Imagine what the impact on his family would have been if the jailer had proceeded with his ill-conceived suicide plan. A wife would have been instantly cut off from her husband's love and support. She would have been forced to relinquish all the joys and privileges of marriage without advance preparation. Lonely children would have found themselves having to work through developmental issues without dad's firm discipline and steady guidance. Finances would have been scarce—the mother might have been forced to work or rely on the state for a meager handout. A stigma would have settled upon the family, for suicide is viewed as an unpopular way to die.

A staggering blow is administered to family, church, and community when someone commits suicide. Conversely, society is spared the heaviness of guilt and disgrace every time a suicide is prevented. Therefore, far-reaching benefits and blessings occur whenever an individual is plucked from the brink of self-destruction.

Suicide is an appalling waste of precious human talent. Suicide foils God's intentions, for man was placed on earth to fellowship with his Lord. "O man . . . what doth the Lord require of thee, but to do justly, and to love mercy, and to walk humbly with thy God?" (Mic. 6:8, KJV). This truth needs to be proclaimed loud and clear: man has been created by God to live—not to die.

It is not necessary for believers to become bogged down with depression and self-destructive ideas. Jesus offers a delightfully joyful life which He invites us to live with enthusiasm. Jesus said, "I am come that they might have life, and that they might have it more abundantly" (John 10:10, KJV).

15

Lessons to Be Learned from Valley Experiences

It is interesting to note the stereotypes people develop about counselors. People commonly say, "You have studied human behavior, and you probably know all the answers to life's perplexing problems. You must really have your own life together."

Perceptions such as these can be very misleading. Counselors are also subject to depression, from marriage and family problems, and from other stresses. Actually, much of the material in this book springs from my personal encounters with discouragement. In fact, I have struggled through a most difficult bout with depression as I worked on pages of this manuscript. It is almost as though God picked out a deep valley to allow me to experience discouragement while writing this book. Of course, one can more readily explain a subject when he has encountered it personally. Consequently, the material contained in this book includes my personal bouts with depression, along with clinical insights and experiences.

People commonly project an attitude about depression that says: Avoid depression at all costs; if you get discouraged, do whatever you can to get over it as quickly as possible. Depressed patients frequently say, "Just give me a pill, a shot, or something, to make these terrible feelings go away." I can identify with this point of view, as I have prayed for release from the pain of discouragement. However, I sincerely believe that valuable lessons can be gained from valley experiences. Therefore, efforts to eradicate depression with a quick-cure chemical or a hastily devised course of shock therapy may not always be the best approach. It makes much better sense to discover what God would teach through valley experiences.

Can anything positive emerge from a bout with depression? Read on to discover some ways in which depression may enrich your life.

1. *Periods of depression invite self-examination.*

Extreme discouragement may be a signal from the Lord, giving you a clear message that something needs to be changed. Depression should cause an individual to take an intense look at his life style. Ask questions such as: "What are the growing edges that I need to work on at this time? What is God trying to tell me through this experience?" Deep discouragement may signify that a relationship needs mending, behavior patterns need altering, or growth should occur in a particular area.

Look back over the causes of depression described earlier. Are you suffering from guilt that needs to be confessed? You may be depressed because of a negative self-image, indicating that you need to improve the way you feel about yourself. The Lord may be asking you to pull out the root of self-pity that is feeding your depression. Do you harbor anger or bitterness toward others? Perhaps your discouragement signals problems in your family that need to be resolved.

One of my growing edges involves learning to accept criticism and negative feedback. I try hard to maintain a facade that says, "I do things pretty well, so please don't criticize my behavior." While I am growing in this area, I must frequently fight discouragement when someone finds fault with me.

A simple formula operates in this situation:

Affirmation of my behavior=encouragement
Criticism of my behavior=discouragement,
                                        or depression

It is natural to feel encouraged when affirmed and discouraged when criticized.
However, it is important to cope with negative feedback because people may not like me
or agree with the way I handle things. Consequently, discouragement which follows criticism signals an area for personal growth.
God is saying: *I am sending discouragement
to reveal growing edges for you to work on.*
Growth through depression is one of life's
most painful processes. However, dueling with
depression by removing agonizing pain without examining underlying causes is like pulling a weed but leaving the root intact. This is
like knocking a bothersome fly from the air,
but not giving a final blow that removes the
pesty insect from your environment. Ignoring root issues is similar to taking aspirin
for a painful toothache, when the abscessed
molar really needs to be yanked out. A more
realistic approach is to examine closely the
growth issues the Lord is calling to your attention. Therefore, the next time depression
strikes, take a look at root causes before you
gulp down an antidepressant pill.
There may be occasions when underlying

causes of depression are difficult to identify. You may come up empty-handed after searching your mind or closely scrutinizing your life for root causes. In such a case, a visit with your doctor, clergyman, or Christian counselor can uncover areas that may escape your conscious awareness.

2. *Depression offers an opportunity to receive ministry from others.*

Most people agree that the ability to express love is a foundational component to good mental health. While it is important to give, a well-adjusted individual also possesses the capacity to receive from others. There are appropriate occasions for reaching out, as well as times to be ministered unto. Swallowing one's pride to request help often leads to gratifying and enriching experiences.

Biblical characters freely received love and support during life's critical moments. Job's comforters did their best to offer admonition and encouragement to their discouraged friend. God tenderly lifted Jonah, Elijah, and David from the throes of depression. Jesus personally touched Peter with some well-timed words of encouragement perfectly suited to His fallen disciple's need.

Swallowing your pride to say, "I need help" allows others the special privilege of offering their love and care. Times of discouragement present possibilities to receive your family's support in a precious way. For instance, on an occasion when I was particularly depressed my wife called the children around and said, "Let's pray for dad; he's really feeling down." Tears flooded my eyes as my wife and children laid their hands on me and prayed that God would lift my low spirits. The support of family members in saying, "We care about you and will stand with you through this difficult time" is a real gift to me.

Love and support should freely flow from the family of God when one of its members experiences a crisis. However, receiving ministry requires openness about one's needs— no one can help unless they know you have a problem. Humbling yourself to say, "I have a need" will almost certainly bring a loving response from God's people.

Allow yourself to be ministered to by your family and fellow believers as you walk through depression's valleys. You will learn what the Lord means when He directs us to "Bear ye one another's burdens, and so fulfil the law of Christ" (Gal. 6:2, KJV). Isn't this what the body of believers is all about?

3. *Depression offers opportunity for spiritual growth.*

Discouraging times can result in a deepening

of a believer's prayer life and a renewed interest in the Scriptures. God is convicting me for my lack of prayer—I don't spend nearly as much time as I should with the Lord when things are going well. Of course, we should not merely use God as a crutch during times of weakness. However, there is a special sense of comfort and solace in the Word, and a relief that comes through tears as a believer pours out his heart to the Lord from the depths of his discouragement.

Depression drives me to my knees and invites me to search the Scriptures as never before. The Psalms take on special meaning as I struggle to overcome discouragement. I identify with David's moods as he described his feelings of disillusionment and depression in the following manner: "Yet I am standing here depressed and gloomy, but I will meditate upon your kindness to this lovely land where the Jordan River flows and Mount Hermon and Mount Mizar stand. . . .

"Yet day by day the Lord also pours out his steadfast love upon me, and through the night I sing his songs and pray to God who gives me life.

" 'O God my Rock,' I cry, 'why have you forsaken me? Why must I suffer these attacks from my enemies?' Their taunts pierce me like a fatal wound; again and again they scoff, 'Where is that God of yours?' But O my soul, don't be discouraged. Don't be upset. Expect God to act! For I know that I shall again have plenty of reason to praise him for all that he will do. He is my help! He is my God!" (Ps. 42:6-11).

4. *Walking through depression teaches me to relinquish my need to be in control.*

I enjoy being in charge of my life. I am most comfortable when I am in control and things are moving according to my whims. Conversely, I become discouraged when life's events escape my sphere of influence.

Problems which drive me to discouragement are frequently those that are entirely out of my control. Since I can do nothing about these irksome situations, my only alternative is to relinquish the reins and trust others. This difficult process can be extremely growth-producing. I am learning new levels of trust as I place my destiny into another person's hands along with divine guidance.

A motto on my desk reads: "God has everything under control." There are times when this saying is easily believable. However, doubts about the reality of this message also sweep over me. Discouraging moments offer occasions when I must grasp the reality that God is "the blessed controller of all things." I can put my situation under His direction because He is truly working in my behalf.

5. *Overcoming depression allows me an opportunity to rise above self-centered behavior patterns.*

I focus on my needs, my problems, and my dilemmas when I am depressed. Every other word becomes "my." How could I ever allow myself to become so self-centered? This process confirms the extent to which I am into my own feelings when I am depressed.

I notice a very important process happening in my life as I break away from discouragement—I am talking less about myself and speaking more about the Lord. Slowly but surely He begins to occupy center stage in the drama of my life. I am on the road to recovery from depression when preoccupation with self disappears and I focus my thoughts on Jesus. Praise His name for the healing process He is accomplishing in my life.

6. *Periods of depression make me more sensitive to the needs of others.*

You can never fully comprehend another person's pain until you go through a similar trial. Alcoholics understand addiction to the bottle; drug addicts have special insights into drug dependence; cancer victims know the shock of a doctor's announcement of that dreadful disease.

Similarly, depression sensitizes me to the hurts of others. I can empathize with the pain of your depression, because I have experienced similar suffering. My counseling ministry is growing to new dimensions of effectiveness as I identify with my client's struggles.

We refer to Jesus as the Great Physician because He empathizes with us when we hurt. The Lord is able to be touched with the feelings of our infirmities because He experienced problems similar to ours (Heb. 4:15). As this sensitizes the Lord to our needs, so we can identify with others who walk through depression's deep valley when we have been there ourselves.

7. *Walking through depression gives a new perspective on life's meaning.*

Are you afraid of people? An innate fear of what others might do to us is frequently at the root of depression. Jesus combats this basic fear with a statement that has helped me deal with my unrealistic fears: "Don't be afraid of those who can kill only your bodies— but can't touch your souls! Fear only God who can destroy both soul and body in hell" (Matt. 10:28).

Assessing what people can snatch away from you may produce some surprising results.

Are you worried about losing material goods? Remember that Jesus claimed nothing as His own during His earthly pilgrimage. "But Jesus said, 'Foxes have dens and birds have nests, but I, the Messiah, have no home of my own—no place to lay my head' " (Matt. 8:20). Are you concerned about your reputation? Recall that Jesus was always willing to take a humble servant's role. "But he made himself of no reputation, and took upon him the form of a servant, and was made in the likeness of men" (Phil. 2:7, KJV).

You can lose your reputation, your health, and your wealth, but no one can snatch away your eternal soul. Your undying spirit is forever hidden with Christ in God. Rejoice in the security that this statement offers you.

Experiencing depression gives a renewed sense of priorities and teaches believers what is really important. Eternal values overshadow the picayune pleasures and material goods that this world offers. Christians can rejoice, for we enjoy the best of both worlds. We can never be a loser, "For to me to live is Christ, and to die is gain" (Phil. 1:21, KJV).

8. *Depression invites believers to cling tenaciously to God's precious promises.*

One needs to hold tightly to God's reassuring message of security during discouraging times. A wonderful promise that has been especially helpful to me when I am depressed is found in Rom. 8:28: "All things work together for good to them that love God" (KJV). What a comfort to realize God is in control of my life and will work out everything for my good.

It is difficult to understand how everything can turn out satisfactorily when I am down. My world seems to turn upside down; everything becomes topsy-turvy. The pieces of my puzzle lay in a helter-skelter fashion, without rhyme or reason. I cannot comprehend how these events could ever work out to my good.

However, deep within me is a hope that I cling to with an unfaltering confidence. From the depths of my being a still, small voice whispers, *"Keep holding on—everything is going to turn out satisfactorily."* I know this is true, because I serve a God who brings hope out of adversity. He snatches victory out of the jaws of defeat. I marvel as the Lord takes the mixed-up pieces of my life and puts them together in a perfectly coherent pattern.

One must look beyond today's events to comprehend fully the depth of meaning concealed in Rom. 8:28. God sees the future; He has a picture of our lives that is difficult to understand at this moment. For instance,

Joseph surely had difficulty comprehending that his pilgrimage into Egypt could turn out positively. Joseph was forsaken by his brothers, falsely accused by Potipher's wife, far removed from family and friends. "How could this ever turn out for my good," Joseph probably wondered as he peered out of prison bars. On the surface, everything seemed to be going wrong. However, Joseph's testimony radically changed as he looked back on his life and victoriously proclaimed, "As far as I am concerned, God turned into good what you meant for evil" (Gen. 50:20).

Let this simple, but profound, saying saturate your thinking: *This too will pass.* A brighter day will dawn for you. The clouds will eventually roll back, and the sunshine of God's love will pour in upon you once again. You can lean hard upon God's precious promises, for He will never fail or let you down. He who has promised to do so will work out all the events of your life for your benefit.

Afterword

A common element emerges as we study biblical characters who experienced depression. Their unshakable faith and trust in God is like a thread that is interwoven into each situation. These individuals may speak of adversity, pressures, sadness, and discouragement in one breath. However, their next sentence rings with confidence and glowing trust in the Lord.

Job had an unshakable confidence that God would see him through his ordeal. Job's famous statement: "Though he slay me, yet will I trust in him," sounds like a clarion call to a Christian to trust God even in life's darkest hour (13:15, KJV). Job's trust in God is underscored further when he testifies, "I know my redeemer liveth" (19:25, KJV).

A once-discouraged David cried out with faith in God, "Take courage, my soul! . . . I shall yet praise him again. . . . day by day the Lord also pours out his steadfast love upon me, and through the night I sing his songs and pray to God who gives me life. 'O God my Rock,' I cry, 'why have you forsaken me?'. . . . Again and again they scoff, 'Where is that God of yours?' But O my soul, don't be discouraged. Don't be upset. Expect God to act! For I know that I shall again have plenty of reason to praise him for all that he will do. He is my help! He is my God!" (Ps. 42:4-11).

Peter, who went through a deep valley after denying the Lord, later proclaimed, "Beloved, think it not strange concerning the fiery trial which is to try you, as though some strange thing happened unto you: But rejoice, inasmuch as ye are partakers of Christ's sufferings; that, when his glory shall be revealed, ye may be glad also with exceeding joy" (1 Pet. 4:12-13, KJV).

Paul mentions being abased and bogged down with discouraging thoughts. However, he bounces back to proclaim with confidence, "I can do all things through Christ which strengtheneth me. . . . And he said unto me, My grace is sufficient for thee, for my strength is made perfect in weakness" (Phil. 4:13, 2 Cor. 12:9, KJV). Paul said further, "We are troubled on every side, yet not distressed; we are perplexed, but not in despair; Persecuted, but not forsaken; cast down, but not destroyed" (2 Cor. 4:8-9).

The key to overcoming depression for a Christian is a steadfast faith and trust in the Lord. You can pin your hopes on Him, realizing He will deliver you. He is with you in sadness and depression as well as during joyful occasions. This unshakable trust in the Lord says, "I know that He will bring me through." Confidence like this will result in victory over depression when your trust is in the Lord.

A young man named John who went through a severe crisis with depression returned for a checkup one year after overcoming his discouragement. When I asked John to specify what brought him out of his crisis, he stated, "The thing that helped me most was recognizing that there was hope for me to overcome my discouragement."

As John was leaving my office, he grasped my hand warmly and said, "Mr. Johnson, keep on telling people there is hope for them to get over depression. Let them know that through faith in God and the encouragement of family and Christian friends, they can overcome their discouragement."

John and I shed many tears as he struggled through his crisis with depression. As we warmly grasped hands for the last time, both of us reached for a handkerchief to shamelessly wipe away tears trickling down our cheeks. We both knew that these were a different kind of tears, for rejoicing had replaced sorrow. We understood more deeply and keenly the insight of the Psalmist when he said, "Weeping may endure for a night, but joy cometh in the morning" (Ps. 30:5, KJV).